MW01224651

SOUND AND SILENCE

SINOTHEORY

A series edited by Carlos Rojas and Eileen Cheng-yin Chow

SOUND AND SILENCE

MY EXPERIENCE WITH CHINA AND LITERATURE

TRANSLATED AND WITH AN INTRODUCTION BY CARLOS ROJAS

DUKE UNIVERSITY PRESS
Durham and London 2024

© 2014 Yan Lianke
© 2024 Introduction and English Translation,
Duke University Press
All rights reserved
Printed in the United States of America on
acid-free paper ∞
Project Editor: Lisa Lawley
Designed by A. Mattson Gallagher
Typeset in Adobe Jensen Pro and Futura Std
by Copperline Book Services

Library of Congress Cataloging-in-Publication Data
Names: 880-01 Yan, Lianke, [date] author. | Rojas, Carlos,
[date] translator.
Title: Sound and silence : my experience with China and
literature / Yan Lianke ; translated by Carlos Rojas.
Other titles: 880-02 Chen mo yu chuan xi. English |
Sinotheory.
Description: Durham : Duke University Press, 2024. |
Series: Sinotheory | Includes bibliographical references
and index.
Identifiers: LCCN 2023033079 (print)
LCCN 2023033080 (ebook)
ISBN 9781478030393 (paperback)
ISBN 9781478026167 (hardcover)
ISBN 9781478059387 (ebook)
Subjects: LCSH: 880-03 Yan, Lianke, 1958—Authorship. |
Chinese literature—History and criticism. | Criticism—
China. | BISAC: LITERARY CRITICISM / Asian / Chinese |
LITERARY CRITICISM / Modern / 21st Century | LCGFT:
Lectures. | Essays. | Speeches.
Classification: LCC PL2925.L54 C4413 2024 (print) |
LCC PL2925.L54 (ebook) | DDC 895.18/5209—dc23/
eng/20231221
LC record available at https://lccn.loc.gov/2023033079
LC ebook record available at https://lccn.loc.gov/2023033080

Cover art: Chen Yu, *Hoping*, 2017. Oil on canvas,
90 × 120 cm. Courtesy of the artist and Schoeni
Projects.

Contents

Acknowledgments

This volume arose out of a series of lectures that the author gave during a trip to North America in the spring of 2014, thanks to an invitation by Duke University professor and scholar Carlos Rojas, who is also the author's English translator. During that trip, the author visited twelve universities, including Duke, Harvard, Yale, and Stanford, where his lectures were recorded and subsequently transcribed and edited. The first essay in this volume was initially delivered as the author's acceptance speech upon being awarded the Franz Kafka Prize in October 2014. The author is grateful to Duke University for helping to coordinate his 2014 lecture tour and to Duke University Press for making this volume available to an English-language readership.

Translator's Introduction

CARLOS ROJAS

Yan Lianke was born in rural Henan, in a community so remote that, to this day, he himself doesn't know his exact birth date. In lieu of the calendar date, his mother simply remembers what the wheat fields looked like on the day of his birth. Two decades later, when Yan needed to specify his birth date while filling out paperwork to join the army, he decided that his mother's description of the wheat field corresponded roughly to what one might see in August, before the late-summer harvest. As for the year, he calculated that her description probably corresponded to the summer of 1958, before the catastrophic crop failures that began to afflict much of the country in 1959.

Coincidentally, the date that Yan ultimately selected as his official birth date, August 24, 1958, happened to fall right in the middle of the 1958 Beidaihe Conference, which ran from August 17 to August 30. At this historic meeting, the Politburo passed a series of resolutions significantly raising steel and grain production targets while also supporting the establishment of people's communes throughout the country — thereby marking the high point of the Great Leap Forward Campaign that Chairman Mao had launched at the beginning of the year. Within months of this conference, however, the Party's wildly unrealistic production targets had backfired, triggering an economic crisis. The nation was subsequently plunged into a devastating famine that is estimated to have claimed tens of millions of lives during the three-year period that official historiography euphemistically calls the "three years of natural disaster," but which is often described simply as the Great Famine. It is fitting that the date Yan selected as his official birth date coincided with the Beidaihe Conference because just as the Great Leap Forward's overly ambitious production goals resulted in almost unimaginable suffering for the Chinese people, many of Yan's fictional works similarly focus on the sufferings of those individuals and communities positioned on society's margins.

Yan's works are noteworthy for his careful attention to writing as a craft. Each of his works since around 1998 adopts a different narrative structure and is written in a different voice. For instance, one novel is narrated in reverse chronological order, beginning with the protagonist's death and then working its way back to his birth, whereas another is narrated mostly from "beyond the grave" in the first-person voice of a boy who had been killed shortly before the novel's fictional starting point. One work consists of four interwoven (fictional) texts, each of which is written in a completely different voice and is reproduced in the novel only in fragmentary fashion, and another interweaves a complex textual narrative with a parallel story told via a series of more than two hundred intricate paper-cut images that Yan commissioned from a paper-cut artist, who spent a year and a half designing and producing the images to meet Yan's specifications. Some of Yan's works parody Chinese socialist discourse, but he also engages dialogically with a wide range of other discourses, ranging from premodern Chinese poetry and drama to Christian religious rhetoric. The result is a remarkable body of work that distinguishes itself by its linguistic and literary innovations, even as he simultaneously uses his literature to offer a unique vision of contemporary China and its people.

In addition to his fictional works, Yan Lianke is also active as an essayist, frequently lecturing and writing on a wide range of topics relating to literature and society. In addition to his literary criticism—and most notably *Discovering Fiction*, his 2011 book-length study on different approaches to literary realism from the nineteenth century to the present—he is particularly interested in the position of authors and artists in contemporary Chinese society and their potential role in observing and reflecting on contemporary conditions. A handful of his essays have been translated into English—including two *New York Times* essays on "state-sponsored amnesia" and on "China's darkness," which were published in 2013 and 2014, respectively.[1]

Yan's state-sponsored-amnesia essay speaks to the phenomenon whereby recent politically sensitive incidents like the Great Famine and the June Fourth Tiananmen Square crackdown have been erased so thoroughly from public discourse in China that many young people are not even aware of their existence. Yan observes that a similar logic also applies to literature and popular culture, resulting in an array of carrot-and-stick strategies that use a combination of "soft" incentives and "hard" coercions to push literary and cultural production away from unwanted topics and toward more desirable ones. In 2013 Yan accepted an offer to teach every spring semester at the Hong Kong University of Science and Technology (HKUST), where he is currently IAS Sin Wai Kin Professor of Chinese Culture and Chair Professor of Humanities. As a result, for the past decade he has been dividing his time between his Hong Kong appointment and his original position at Renmin University in Beijing, where he has been serving as professor of the School of Liberal Arts since 2004. At the same time, given the growing restrictions on publishing his works in China, he has increasingly come to rely on publishing houses in Hong Kong and Taiwan to publish the Chinese-language versions of his works, and on presses around the world to publish his works in translation—and, to date, his works have been translated into more than thirty languages.

In his 2013 *New York Times* essay, Yan observes that the Chinese state regularly uses its financial and regulatory influence to encourage writers and artists to work within politically acceptable parameters. For instance, he notes that "almost all awards in China in the fields of literature, art, news and culture are administered within state-approved boundaries," and although it is true that Yan himself has won many of China's top literary prizes, including the Lu Xun Literature Prize (twice) and the Lao She Literature Prize, in the last decade or so he has primarily been recognized by numerous international literary institutions. His most prestigious international accolades include the 2013 Hua Zong World Literature Prize (from Malaysia), the 2014 Franz Kafka Prize (from the Czech Republic), the 2016 Dream of the Red Chamber Award (from Hong Kong), and the 2021 Newman Prize for Chinese Literature (from the United States). In 2021 he was named one of the twelve inaugural RSL International Writers recognized by Britain's Royal Society of Literature. Yan was also twice a finalist (in 2013 and 2016) for the Man Booker International Prize.

Yan's 2014 essay on "China's darkness" was an abbreviated version of the acceptance speech that he had delivered upon being awarded the Kafka Prize in October of that year. Established in 2001, the Franz Kafka Prize has twice, in 2004 and 2005, recognized authors who went on to win the Nobel Prize later that same year.[2] The Kafka Prize recognizes authors whose work is distinguished by "its humanistic character and contribution to cultural, national, language and religious tolerance, its existential, timeless character, its generally human validity and its ability to hand over a testimony about our times."[3]

Although Yan made no direct reference to Kafka's work in his acceptance speech for the Kafka Prize, this was certainly not for lack of familiarity. In *Discovering Fiction*, for instance, Yan includes a lengthy discussion of the formative impact that Kafka's fiction had not only on his own literary development but also on that of other major twentieth-century authors. In that earlier volume, Yan also identifies Kafka's work, and particularly "The Metamorphosis," as marking a crucial turning point between nineteenth-century realism and the twentieth-century modernist experiments that helped lay the groundwork for Yan's own current narrative style, which he calls mythorealism (*shenshizhuyi*)—he explains that this is a mode of realism wherein the work's relationship to reality "is not driven by direct causality, but instead involves a person's soul and spirit (which is to say, the connection between a person, on one hand, and the real relationship between spirit and interior objects, on the other), and an author's conjectures grounded on a real foundation."[4]

Rather than address Kafka directly in his acceptance speech, Yan instead proposes a Kafkaesque allegory of a blind man from Yan's hometown who always took a flashlight with him when he went out at night. As Yan explains, the function of the flashlight was not to help the blind man see his surroundings but to help *other* villagers see the blind man, and in the process hopefully see the darkness that the blind man sees. This allegory reflects a recurrent theme in Yan's work, in which he uses darkness to characterize not only the societal conditions reflected in his works but also his works' objectives and conditions of production. He believes that contemporary China is marked by metaphorical darkness, and he tries to use his writings to help his readers to perceive that same darkness. His goal, in other words, is not to help his readers see *in* the darkness but to enable them to perceive the darkness itself.

In spring of 2014, a few months before he was awarded the Franz Kafka Prize, Yan embarked on a North American lecture tour to promote the recent publication of the English translation of his 2004 novel *Shouhuo* (translated as *Lenin's Kisses*). This was the third of Yan's novels to be published in English translation, and the preceding two were both works that had been banned in China. For instance, the original version of his 2005 novella *Serve the People!* had been serialized in a mainland China literary journal but was subsequently banned before it could be released in book form. Similarly, Yan had subjected the original version of his 2006 novel *Dream of Ding Village* to a rigorous process of self-censorship to avoid a similar fate, but the mainland Chinese edition ended up being banned shortly after its initial publication anyway. Also, although *Lenin's Kisses* was published openly in China in 2004, its publication nevertheless led to Yan's being asked to leave the People's Liberation Army (PLA), which had been his employer since 1977. (Yan was subsequently able to secure a faculty position teaching literature and creative writing at Beijing's Renmin University.)

All three of the preceding works focus on dark aspects of contemporary China and its recent history. *Serve the People!* is set in the Cultural Revolution and features an adulterous affair that combines libidinal desire with political fervor, *Dream of Ding Village* reflects on contemporary China's rural HIV/AIDS epidemic and underscores the degree to which the crisis was exacerbated by local profiteering, and *Lenin's Kisses* features a plotline in which the disabled residents of a remote village are forced to travel the country performing their own disabilities for profit. At the same time, the way in which these works were subjected to a combination of external censorship and self-censorship reflects what is arguably an even darker facet of contemporary Chinese society—an issue to which Yan sometimes alludes allegorically in his fictional works, but which he addressed head-on in several of the talks he gave during his 2014 lecture tour. For instance, in the talk he gave at Duke University as part of that same tour, Yan noted that when he travels abroad he is often introduced as "China's most controversial and most censored author." This was already true in 2014, when Yan delivered the lecture in question, and it is even more so today (currently, China's publication restrictions apply not only to Yan's most recent works but also to many of his earlier ones). Though recognizing that some readers may view this "banned in China" label as an attractive selling point (in that it promises a view of China that the state wants to suppress), Yan says that he feels ambivalent about the designation. He notes that whereas it is true that some great works of literature have been banned, one could nevertheless also cite countless mediocre works that have similarly been banned—suggesting that there is no necessary correlation between being banned and being a great work of art. On the other hand, Yan also observes that, given contemporary China's mercurial publication policies, for a contemporary Chinese author to *never* encounter problems with the censorship apparatus would itself be grounds for suspicion.

The Kafka Prize is open to authors writing in any language, but one of the prize's eligibility requirements is that the nominees must have published at least two books that were either written in or translated into Czech. A Czech-language version of *Serve the People!* was published in 2008. The second of Yan's novels to be translated into Czech—and consequently the work that technically made him fully eligible for the Kafka Prize—was *The Four Books* (the translation was completed in 2014 and was released in 2015). First published in Chinese in 2011, not only was the novel banned in China, but furthermore it is centrally concerned with issues of literary restrictions. The novel is set in a political reeducation camp for intellectuals during the Anti-Rightist Campaign of the late 1950s. One character in the work, a mysterious figure known only as "the Child" who runs the camp, routinely confiscates and burns all the detainees' personal books—including both Chinese and foreign volumes. However, the novel concludes with the revelation that even as the Child had been routinely confiscating and burning the detainees' books, he was also secretly collecting extra copies of each of these titles for his own private collection.

The book that Yan had completed just before embarking on his 2014 North American lecture tour was his 2013 novel *The Explosion Chronicles*. The work's plot, like that of *The Four Books*, revolves around themes of censorship and book burning. In particular, the novel describes how the protagonist, a Beijing-based author named Yan Lianke, is recruited by local officials to compile a local gazetteer detailing the history of his former hometown. What had originally been a modest village undergoes explosive growth during the post-Mao Reform Era, being quickly redesignated as a town, city, and eventually a megalopolis. After the novel's fictional Yan Lianke completes his assignment, however, the local official who had originally commissioned the work expresses his dissatisfaction with the text's portrayal of his community and retaliates by burning the manuscript as the protagonist watches in horror.

The theme of book burning is symbolically powerful in almost any context, but in a Chinese context it is particularly resonant, given that it is recorded that one of the first acts of Qin Shi Huang, China's first emperor, after unifying the Chinese nation in 221 BCE, was ordering that almost all the country's books be burned (books on medicine, divination, agriculture, and forestry were excepted). However, both *The Four Books* and *The Explosion Chronicles* introduce an intriguing twist to this theme of book burning. Just as in *The Four Books* it is revealed that the Child had been amassing a vast private collection by secretly keeping a copy of virtually every title he confiscated and burned, similarly in *The Explosion Chronicles* the disclosure that the local official burns the fictional Yan Lianke's manuscript is seemingly contravened by the suggestion that the novel is itself a version of the local historiography destroyed by the local official. In both cases, themes of destruction and censorship are inextricably intertwined with corresponding motifs of creation and appreciation, and it is precisely in the interstices of these two sets of tendencies that Yan's own contemporary work is positioned.

Although Yan's works are now available in translation to readers around the world, Yan nevertheless insists that his primary audience has always been his fellow Chinese. He knows no language other than Chinese. In this respect, the essays in *Sound and Silence* are unusual in that they were composed specifically for foreign audiences. Some of the pieces echo concerns that Yan has raised in similar fora in China, but others speak directly to the difficulties he has encountered within China and the ways he is perceived abroad. Another concern that runs through the volume involves Yan's perception of foreign society and culture, and particularly his views on foreign literature. Yan has read many foreign literary works in translation, and in several of these essays he offers detailed commentaries on literary works from Europe, North America, and Japan.

The present collection of essays opens with the full text of the acceptance speech Yan presented at the Franz Kafka Prize award ceremony in October 2014, and the other essays are based on the lectures he gave during his North American tour in the spring of that same year.

A slightly different version of this volume was published in Chinese in Taiwan in August 2014, but without the Kafka Prize acceptance speech. Many of the lectures on which the essays in this volume are based were rather colloquial, and here we have retained some of these conversational elements while also lightly editing the essays for concision and clarity. For instance, Yan, who is known for his self-deprecating humor, frequently alternates the point of view in these essays, referring to himself in the first, second, and third person—sometimes shifting from one usage to another even in the same sentence. In this volume we have retained some of these pronoun shifts where the referent was clear from the context (such as when Yan refers to himself in the third person to describe what other people are saying about him), but we have silently modified others where they seemed potentially confusing to readers. We have refrained from adding editorial footnotes to preserve the feel of the original essays and have adopted a very light hand in silently adding minor supplementary material to the translated essays (for instance, Yan refers to many Western authors only by their last name, but we have often added their first name, in accordance with English-language academic conventions). Above all, we have attempted to retain the powerful storytelling qualities of the original talks.

Indeed, one of Yan Lianke's strengths is his skill as a storyteller, and his most recent novel was released in 2021 in China under the title *Central Plains* (*Zhongyuan*) but in Taiwan under the title *A Chinese Story* (*Zhongguo gushi*). Yan Lianke wrote the first draft of the work between January and April of 2020, as China was facing its first wave of COVID-19 infections, and although the novel—which features a cycle of stories by a husband, wife, and son, who fantasize about killing one another—does not directly address the pandemic, it nevertheless reflects on issues of life, death, narrative orientation, and geographic constraint that played a critical role during the crisis. Coincidentally, it was also in the first months of 2020 that President Xi Jinping took the "tell the good China story" slogan he had first introduced in 2013 and retooled it to urge the Chinese people "to tell the good China story of fighting the pandemic." In so doing, Xi was concerned not only with shaping how China would be viewed by the rest of the world but also how the Chinese people would view the biopolitical measures that the state was enacting in response to the crisis.

Just months after publishing the Taiwan edition of *A Chinese Story*, meanwhile, Yan had the opportunity to offer his own story on the pandemic itself. On February 21, 2022, he delivered the first lecture for an online class he was teaching at HKUST (like many academics around the world, Yan had been teaching his classes online since 2020 because of the pandemic), and the text of his preliminary remarks was quickly posted to many online fora. In particular, Yan opened his lecture by asking his students, "Do you have the capacity for memory?" He explained that "having the capacity for memory is the soil for memory itself, as memory grows and extends from this soil. Having memory and the capacity for memory is the fundamental difference that distinguishes humans from animals." Yan then invited his students to consider the following counterfactual scenario:

> Imagine for a moment that we don't discuss those distant histories that have already undergone a change of book cover and book number, and instead focus only on events from the past twenty years, which young people like yourselves, who were born in the 1980s and 1990s, have experienced and can remember, including the national crises such as AIDS, SARS, and the novel coronavirus. Are these latter crises man-made disasters, or are they natural disasters that humans are unable to resist, like the Tangshan and Wenchuan earthquakes?

Yan concludes by observing that even though it may be difficult to identify the precise cause of the present crisis, at the very least we can ask "Where did our memories of these earlier crises go?"[5] The title of Yan's speech captures his conclusion: "After this plague, let us become people with memory."

Although societal memory has long been an important concern for Yan, in his 2020 lecture he focuses not only on individual and collective memory (*jiyi*) but rather on the very *capacity* for memory (*jixing*). Moreover, Yan's focus on memory and amnesia in the context of the pandemic is very fitting, given that a key factor in the virus's ability to spread through communities is whether a sufficiently large percentage of the population had developed resistance or immunity—meaning that someone's immune system retains a memory of previous inoculations or infections that can permit it to respond more effectively to future infections. Similarly, in this 2022 talk, and throughout most of his career, Yan has persistently attempted to help his readers "see the darkness" and to spur their "capacity for memory"—in order to better position them not only to remember previous traumas or crises but also to respond more effectively to future ones.

NOTES

1 Yan Lianke, "On China's State-Sponsored Amnesia," trans. Jane Weizhen Pan and Martin Merz, *New York Times*, April 1, 2013; Yan Lianke, "Finding Light in China's Darkness," trans. Carlos Rojas, *New York Times*, October 23, 2014.

2 The future Nobel laureates in question were Elfriede Jelinek and Harold Pinter.

3 After being awarded annually from 2001 to 2020, the prize now appears to have been discontinued. The statement here is from the webpage of the Franz Kafka Society, which is offline but has been archived. Franz Kafka Society, "Der Franz-Kafka-Preis" [The Franz Kafka Prize], archived January 11, 2022, at Archive.org, https://web.archive.org/web/20220111121858/http://franzkafka-soc.cz/cena-franze-kafky/.

4 Yan Lianke, *Discovering Fiction*, trans. Carlos Rojas (Durham, NC: Duke University Press, 2021), 99.

5 Yan Lianke, 經此疫劫, 讓我們成為有記性的人 ("Jing ci yijie, rang women chengwei you jixing de ren" [After this plague, let us become people with memory]), *China Digital Times*, February 22, 2020.

1 He Who Has Been Selected by Heaven and Life to Appreciate Darkness

We could say that as authors we live for the sake of our memories and feelings, just as it is those same memories and feelings that transform us into authors.

It is for this reason that, as I stand here before you today, I am reminded how half a century ago, between 1960 and 1962, China's efforts to promote socialism resulted in what is known as the Three Years of Natural Disaster, during which more than thirty million people starved to death. One evening after the beginning of this devastating "man-made" catastrophe, I was living in our family's poor and isolated village in central China, which was surrounded by a protective wall built during the war. I was only a child at the time, and I followed my mother as she went to dump our garbage outside the village wall. Holding my hand, my mother pointed to the white clay and yellow earth along the top of the wall and said, "Son, you must always remember that when people are starving to death, they can eat this white clay and elm-tree bark. However, if they try to eat yellow earth or the bark of any other kind of tree, they will die even faster."

Mother then went back inside to cook some food, leaving behind a shadow like dried-up leaves blowing in the wind. Meanwhile, I remained standing on that edible clay gazing out at the sunset, the village, and the fields as an enormous sheet of darkness gradually approached.

From that point on, I proceeded to develop a keen appreciation for darkness.

From that point on, I've always remembered the word *suffering*, which for me refers to the torment one endures under the shadow of darkness.

During that period, whenever I felt hungry and would tug at my mother's hand begging for food, she needed only utter the word *suffering*, and I would immediately see a sheet of murky darkness.

During that period, Chinese New Year's was traditionally a day of celebration for all children. One time, however, my father, upon seeing me and my siblings smile as the festive day approached, softly uttered the word *suffering*, at which point I immediately slipped away and hid alone in the darkness. Never again did I get excited at the approach of New Year's.

During that period, the Chinese people's primary concern was not with survival, but rather with revolution. But when revolution required that my parents raise a red flag and march down the streets shouting, "Long Live Chairman Mao!" my parents and their fellow villagers turned their backs on revolution and, in despair, uttered the word *suffering*. As for me, whenever I heard that word, I would always see a sheet of darkness unfold before me, as though night had suddenly descended in the middle of the day.

As a result, I came to understand that darkness is not just a color but life itself. Darkness is the Chinese people's fate, as well as their means of relating to that fate. I subsequently joined the army and left that isolated village, leaving behind that piece of land where I was born and raised. But no matter what subsequently happened, I would always see a sheet of darkness stretched out before me. I would stand behind that dark curtain, using my ability to endure darkness in order to resist it, just as I used my ability to endure hardship in order to resist it.

Of course, today's China is no longer the China of yesteryear. It has now become rich and powerful, and because it has solved the basic problem of providing 1.3 billion people with food, clothing, and spending money, it therefore resembles a bright ray of light illuminating the global East. But beneath this ray of light there lies a dark shadow. It is as if the brighter the light, the darker the shadow, and the darker the shadow, the thicker the corresponding sheet of darkness. Some people experience warmth, brightness, and beauty under that ray of light, whereas others, because they are naturally anxious and depressed, feel the cold darkness that lies beneath.

As for me, I am one of those people who is fated to experience darkness. Therefore, when I look at contemporary China, I see a nation that is thriving yet distorted, developing yet mutated. I see corruption, absurdity, disorder, and chaos. Every day, something occurs that lies outside ordinary reason and logic. A system of morality and a respect for humanity that developed over several millennia is now unraveling and collapsing, as if the yardstick of the law had become a mere child's toy. Today, if one adopts an author's perspective to discuss the nation's institutions together with issues of power, freedom, belief, reality, and so forth, one will inevitably fall short. For such an author, because of these countless things that continue to deteriorate, people are concerned mostly with securing food, drink, housing, and transportation, as well as issues of health care, reproduction, birth, and aging. In that author's eyes, things have never been as gloomy and depressing as they are today, nor have they been as terrifying and exciting. Everyone is simultaneously awaiting but also dreading something, like a critically ill patient awaiting the arrival of an illusory new medicine—hoping that the medicine will arrive soon but at the same time worrying that in the process it will destroy the state of expectation that has sustained the patient up to that point. This sort of uneasy and fearful expectation has produced an unprecedented collective sense of anxiety. For such an author, this collective anxiety becomes a dark shadow in that site of greatest brightness, becoming the other side of the enormous curtain lying beneath those bright rays.

No one can tell such an author where the nation's speeding locomotive of economic development will end up.

No one can tell such an author whether the various political movements and revolutions that have enveloped the nation up to the present day will hover over everyone's head like dark clouds, thunder, or a bolt of lightning capable of piercing the clouds.

Moreover, now that money and power have replaced socialism and capitalism, and society has abandoned the ideals of democracy, freedom, law, and morality, no one can tell such an author what kind of price should be paid for human emotion, human nature, and human dignity.

I remember how, more than a decade ago, I went several times to visit an AIDS village in my home province of Henan. The village had more than eight hundred residents, of whom more than two hundred were infected with HIV. Most of the infected were workers between the ages of thirty and forty-five, the vast majority of whom had become infected because they had gone together to sell blood, in hopes of getting rich and improving their lives. Death became as frequent and inevitable as the setting sun, and the village eventually became so dark that it seemed as though the sun had disappeared permanently from the sky. Whenever I glimpsed a blinding ray of light, everything immediately became enveloped in a shadowy darkness from which I could not escape.

I knew that in that vast land full of chaos and vitality, I was superfluous.

I knew that in that vast land full of chaos and vitality, I was but a superfluous author.

Yet I was also convinced that in that vast land full of chaos and vitality, my writings could come to have an irreplaceable significance. This is because—given that I'm destined to be someone who can appreciate only darkness—I'm like the child who noticed that the emperor was wearing no clothes. Under the light of the sun, I constantly observe pockets of shadows beneath the trees, just as during every joyous ode, I always stand off to one side. When everyone else says it is warm, I always feel it is bitter cold, and when everyone else says that it is bright, I see nothing but darkness. When everyone else is joyfully singing and dancing, I notice that someone has tied a rope to their feet and is about to pull them all down and tie everyone up. I see that in the depths of the people's souls there is unthinkable evil, and I recognize the humiliation that intellectuals must endure in order to stand up and think for themselves. I understand that the spiritual lives of countless ordinary Chinese are being shattered by power even as they are surrounded by money and music.

I'm reminded of a blind man from my village who lived to the age of seventy. Every morning when the sun came up, he would turn to the eastern mountains and, facing the rising sun, would say to himself, "It turns out that sunlight is actually black—but that is good!"

Even in winter, when the blind man was warming himself in the sunlight, he would smile and say, "The darker it gets, the warmer it becomes!"

Even more remarkably, ever since he was young, this blind man always had several flashlights, and whenever he went out at night he would always take one with him. The darker it got, the longer and brighter the beam from his flashlight would become. As a result, as he was walking through the village streets in the middle of the night, people would be able to see him coming and wouldn't run into him. Furthermore, when people encountered him, he would use his flashlight to illuminate the road in front of them. To commemorate this blind man after his death, when his family and the other villagers went to pay their respects and offer gifts, they all offered flashlights full of fresh batteries. As a result, his coffin was filled with flashlights.

Inspired by this blind man, I developed a new form of writing that is premised on a conviction that the darker it is, the brighter it becomes, and the colder it is, the warmer it becomes. The entire significance of this sort of writing lies in permitting people to avoid its existence. My writing, in other words, is like the blind man with the flashlight who shines his limited light into the darkness to help others see the darkness—and thereby to have a target to avoid.

As an important Asian literary ecosystem within world literature, Chinese literature has never before encountered a world and a reality that is so full of optimism but also so full of pessimism. Never before has Chinese literature encountered, in such a remarkably rich, absurd, and strange reality, so many stories and legends—a most ordinary surreality that is simultaneously utterly real and utterly gloomy. There is no comparable period of Chinese history when there has been so much brightness but also so much darkness and obstruction. It is as though contemporary China is not only the light for the entire world but also an enormous source of darkness and anxiety. Meanwhile, the people of China are living in a constant state of fervor and unrest, of timidity and impetuousness. They view history with a combination of fear and dismissal, they view the future with a combination of anticipation and anxiety, and they view contemporary reality as something that is astonishing, unnatural, and illogical yet at the same time something that has a truth, internal logic, and mythoreal absurdity, complexity, and disordered reality that are invisible to ordinary people. In today's China, this disordered reality constitutes a shadow under the greatest brightness and a darkness in the site of greatest light.

In the context of·today's China's history and contemporary reality, when authors see a bright light, that is reality, and when they hear a melodious song, that is also reality. Nihilism and aestheticism are also part of that reality. China's reality is like an enormous forest, with sunlight, vegetation, birds, and streams all being part of that reality. In this forest, dozens and even hundreds of notable authors find a China that is rich and distorted, complicated and contradictory, flourishing yet lacerated. These authors may then use this China as a basis for their writing. As for me, however, I differ from others in that I am somehow fated to see only darkness. I see the dense fog in the depths of the forest and perceive the chaos, the poison, and the terror that lies in that fog. That is to say, whereas others may perceive the beauty of the forest in the daylight, I instead see the darkness and fear of the forest in the middle of the night.

I know that this darkness not only corresponds to a specific time, place, and event but also encompasses the water, air, humans, human emotions, and their ordinary existence. It would be too narrow a reading to claim that darkness includes only the former, for true darkness is that which everyone sees but insists is actually brightness and warmth. The ultimate darkness lies in people's ability to grow accustomed to that same darkness, and the most terrifying darkness occurs when people forget that there was ever light to begin with. It is here that we find literature's potential, given that only literature can help us to find the delicate light, beauty, warmth, and love that lie hidden in the darkness. Therefore, I have dedicated myself to trying to find signs of life within this darkness—to finding light, beauty, warmth, and sympathy.

Accordingly, by transcending time, place, and event, I can perceive the most mundane darkness within contemporary reality. For instance, China may boast of having several thousand years of civilization, but when an old man collapses in the street, everyone refrains from helping him out of fear of being implicated, even as the old man bleeds warm, red blood.

Accordingly, when a pregnant woman dies on the delivery table, the medical technicians all flee to avoid responsibility, leaving behind a tiny soul feebly gasping and crying.

Accordingly, after my home in Beijing was demolished, I experienced a most mundane but also most intense darkness. In this rich and advanced nation, the people who are forcibly relocated in the name of development often have no choice but to protest in the streets because they have nowhere else to turn. When they are rescued after attempting to commit mass suicide by ingesting poison, they are then arrested on charges of "causing trouble." But when someone claims that their suicide was in fact an "elaborate plot," everyone quickly forgets the new troubles and difficulties that ordinary people continue to encounter, together with the darkness that lies beneath the brightness that they enjoy.

I understand that sometimes China's elderly may, in response to some incident, spontaneously commit mass suicide. They kill themselves not because of poverty, disease, exhaustion, or morality but rather because of a deep-rooted sense of anxiety about life, uncertainty about fate, and hopelessness about the contemporary world. When I encounter this sort of incident, the persistent darkness that hovers over everything proceeds to permeate my heart, my life, and my writings. I have my own way of perceiving reality and can use this darkness only to write about that reality. I am unable to open a window and see the world's light, just as I am unable to appreciate—in the midst of the chaos and absurdity of contemporary reality and history—the power of order and human existence. I am always surrounded by chaotic darkness, but it is only from within this darkness that I am thereby able to appreciate the world's light and people's precarious existence.

You could even say that I am a person of darkness. I am an independent writer of darkness and a specter of writing who is hated by light and is driven away from everywhere.

I am reminded of Job, in the Old Testament, who, after experiencing countless misfortunes, asked his wife as she was cursing him, "Shall we accept good from God, and not trouble?" This simple response demonstrates that Job understood that his suffering was merely God's way of testing him, and this was evidence that darkness and light must exist together. As for me, I certainly don't pretend to have been specifically selected by God, as Job was, to endure suffering, but I do know that I am somehow fated to perceive darkness. I hide in the shadows at the periphery of the light, and from these shadows and darkness I perceive the world and lift my pen to write. From these shadows and darkness, I search for light and warmth. I search for love, goodness, and a perpetually beating heart. Through my writing, I attempt to progress from darkness into light.

As an author who believes in literature, regardless of whether I exist as a person or as an author, I am fated to be uneasy because I perceive darkness within the light. For this reason, I am grateful that my father-land is gradually becoming more open and tolerant, to the point that even someone like myself, who is fated to experience only darkness, can be permitted to exist and to write, and can be permitted to stand be-hind the curtain and experience reality, history, and humanity. It is also for this reason that I am particularly grateful to the jurors of the Franz Kafka Prize, who this year have chosen to award me this pure and pris-tine literature prize. Your decision to award me this prize resembles not so much God granting Job riches after he endured a lifetime of suffer-ing, but rather the gesture of awarding a lamp to that blind man walking down the road at night. Because this lamp exists, the blind man who is fated to see only darkness can therefore believe that in front of him there is light. Moreover, it is thanks to this light that people can therefore per-ceive the existence of darkness and consequently more effectively ward off that same darkness and suffering. Meanwhile, that blind man can re-main on the night road, and as people walk past him, he can illuminate the road in front of them—even if just for a short distance.

2 National Amnesia and Literary Memory

I once wrote an essay titled "National Amnesia," in which I recounted how, while in Hong Kong in March of 2012, I met Swedish Sinologist Torbjörn Lodén, who told me how, when he was teaching at the City College of Hong Kong, he once asked his class of more than forty students from China, all of whom were born in the 1980s, "Have any of you heard of June Fourth, Liu Binyan, or Fang Lizhi?" However, the students simply gazed at one another in silence. In response to this story, I told Lodén about another Hong Kong professor who once asked her Chinese students, "Did you know that between thirty and forty million people starved to death during the so-called Three Years of Natural Disaster?" Her students were dumbfounded, reacting as though she had suddenly started to invent Chinese history from scratch to attack the students' rising Chinese nation.

When we had this conversation, Professor Lodén and I were sitting in a quiet Vietnamese restaurant, and after recounting our respective anecdotes, we silently gazed at each other for a long time. From that point on, an issue that people have long privately recognized but never openly discussed became wedged in my brain—this being the problem of national amnesia. I would periodically remember things or dimly hear the blood flowing through my body, whereupon issues relating to national amnesia would gallop through my veins like a herd of horses, arriving at my plaza of self-reproach.

Is it not the case that those Chinese born in the 1980s and 1990s—and who now are in their twenties and thirties—have truly become a generation without memory? Who is it that forced them to forget? How were they made to forget? What responsibility do those of us who are older, and who still retain our memories, have for this younger generation?

Upon reflecting for a while on these issues, I realized that this kind of forgetting could be more accurately called a form of amnesia. This is because the act of forgetting simply means that the past has been left out of one's memory, whereas amnesia connotes a process of selectively excising specific facets of reality or history, combined with the simultaneous construction of *new* memories. Indeed, it is precisely through this amnesiac condition that our nation has managed to leave an entire new generation in what would appear to be a persistent vegetative state. History and reality, the past and the present, are in the process of being actively forgotten—thoroughly erased from the memories of an entire generation. Memory and amnesia, truth and forgetting—these words and phrases are constantly colliding inside our heads. In the past, we believed that history and collective memory would ultimately win out over any short-term memory loss, thereby allowing one to return to an intuitive truth. However, the reality is precisely the opposite. In contemporary China, amnesia inevitably overpowers memory, just as falsity overcomes truth and fabrication becomes the interface that links history and logic. Even things that we just witnessed today end up being cast aside, leaving behind only broken shards of reality and fiction embedded within society, life, and people's brains. And when something unexpected happens tomorrow, these shards will be tossed into a basket of amnesia, which will then be hung in a dark corner out of sight.

WHY ARE THINGS FORGOTTEN?

It must be acknowledged that after the birth of our country, in 1949, revolutionary movements swept over this great nation on a nearly daily basis. Revolution creates political power, history, reality, and even memory itself. Meanwhile, memory and what is remembered, together with natural and forced amnesia, all fall under the category of national memory and national amnesia, thereby becoming a kind of revolutionary choice and method that can be systematically implemented. Here we won't speak of the feudal period, when China was ruled by kings and emperors. Similarly, the Xinhai Revolution that brought down China's last dynasty is now but a distant memory, and while Sun Yat-sen's name is still well-known today, the pivotal historical events that were associated with him have all been selectively excised from our history books and textbooks. Even the old people who lived through China's warlord period and the Sino-Japanese War, and who sacrificed on behalf of different parties, armies, and leaders during the civil war and the anti-Japanese War—they have also been selectively forgotten. This process of forgetting is a national strategy.

Later, when one man's fervor and madness led the entire nation to a frothy state of revolution and construction, the nation initially used mass movements to extend a state of war. After revolution replaced production, there was the 1951 Three Antis Campaign (targeting corruption, waste, and bureaucracy) and the 1953 Five Antis Campaign (targeting graft, tax evasion, theft of state property, theft of economic information, and cheating on government contracts). Looking back now, it is clear that the latter campaign was the most realistic of the countless revolutionary movements that developed in China after 1949. However, because of the revolutionaries' fervor and the fact that this wartime generation inherited the lesson that "political power comes from the muzzle of a gun," the campaign was also very popular and far-reaching. Many places were assigned quotas for the number of people who needed to be seized and supervised, and the issue was not *whether* these places had any revolutionary targets but rather that they *had to have* these revolutionary targets. These pivotal 1951 and 1953 political campaigns laid the foundation for the disastrous 1957 Anti-Rightist Campaign, the mere mention of which still makes Chinese intellectuals quake in fear. The latter event was subsequently removed from everyone's warehouse of memory, and from that point on people were no longer able to discuss—or even mention—it.

Later developments, including the Great Leap Forward, the Great Iron-Smelting Campaign, the so-called Three Years of Natural Disaster (during which between thirty and forty million people starved to death), and the decade-long Cultural Revolution, were so absurd and tragic that they left the entire world dumbfounded. For this reason, people did not dare, were not able, and were not willing to return to these memories so that their children might have an accurate historical image. After China's Reform and Opening Up Campaign, there was the war with Vietnam—no one knew exactly how the war started, and regardless of how many soldiers or civilians died in the conflict, no one ever uttered a word about it. Under the 1983 Strike Hard Campaign, the so-called law—which is merely power grinding its teeth—dictated that countless young lovers were designated as hooligans and imprisoned for merely kissing in public, and countless poor people who had stolen out of desperation were executed.

Of course, the rest of the world remembers the 1989 June Fourth student movement as though it happened just yesterday, and even after the gunshots, bloodshed, and deaths became mere echoes, the details of the event remain etched in the world's collective memory. However, in the country where this event occurred, everyone is wrapped up in the rapid growth of the nation's economy and power, and consequently they have become estranged from the event itself and have even begun to forget that it ever happened. For many who witnessed the crackdown, the memories have come to resemble ethereal, otherworldly dreams. As for the youths who participated in the protests, regardless of whether they subsequently achieved success in life, they all now summarize their experience in one word: "Stupid!" With this, they mock their own earlier behavior and satisfy the demand for amnesia, having already cut off and covered up their individual fate, their collective memory, and their national memory.

What else? There is also everything that is happening today, including the rural HIV/AIDS epidemic; the 2007 Shaanxi Black Brick Kiln incident; multiple gas explosions; tainted dumplings, milk powder, eggs, and seafood; illegally recycled cooking oil; and fruits and vegetables contaminated by carcinogenic additives. There are also the compulsory abortions that were performed under the One-Child policy, the ubiquitous forced demolitions throughout today's cities and countryside, as well as the unethical and illegal persecution of people peacefully petitioning for redress. All these negative incidents with the potential to harm the nation's image and power become reduced to smoke through a system of compulsory amnesia. Following a process of censorship and excision from all newspapers, magazines, television, the internet, and other sites that might contain concrete memories, the objectives of collective amnesia have been attained.

Amnesia is not a special characteristic of everyone's symptoms and ideology; rather, it is a necessary outcome of a national strategy and a social structure. Its most effective vector is through regulations and other methods covering an ideological restriction of speech and the use of power to cut off all conduits through which memory can be preserved—including history books, textbooks, literary works, and other forms of cultural expression. The former Peking University professor Zhang Zhongxing once remarked, "If we can't speak, we can always remain silent. Even if we don't know what to say, we nevertheless always know what *not* to say." Late in life, Professor Fei Xiaotong went to visit Yang Jiang, the wife of the author Qian Zhongshu, and as Fei Xiaotong was leaving the couple's home, Yang Jiang remarked, "You are old now, so you shouldn't keep trying to 'buck the wind.'" Today, this remark might sound like a mere pleasantry, but at the time it also connoted the deep bitterness of the Chinese intellectuals' silence. Sometimes we claim that "silence is a form of voiceless resistance," although in reality silence is simply silence. The same way that if you don't speak for a long time, you may become mute, if you remain silent for a long time, acquiescent silence may similarly become part of your identity and one of the pernicious measures by which the nation enforces its collective amnesia—as the nation becoming a facilitator of those who subject you to obligatory amnesia.

Once an entire people falls silent, the nation itself may also lose its memory. This is not specific to any particular nation, but rather it applies to all nations operating under a dictatorship or centralized state power, or those that find themselves in a period of centralized power, and will use these sorts of strictures to suppress speech. First, the state will silence intellectuals, who tend to have good recall, and will strip them of their memories. Next, as the state gradually consolidates its power, it will extend this amnesiatic state to the general population. Once the next generation knows nothing about this process, this kind of forced amnesia will be able to declare victory, and history will have been completely rewritten.

WAYS OF FORGETTING

Compulsory amnesia may be viewed as a form of rape. The rapist's violence does not have any new significance—unlike an animal staking out its territory that it needs to survive. Meanwhile, the reason why power is able—at an ideological level—to subject reality and history to a form of compulsory amnesia is precisely because power needs to consolidate itself. However, in contemporary China compulsory amnesia cannot be reduced to issues of nation and power, but rather we must also attend to the intellectuals' own complicity in this process. Intellectuals will voluntarily sacrifice their memory—and when they finally reach the complete amnesia that power demands, this is where we find the biggest difference between intellectuals in China and in other countries. For instance, during the White Terror period, the Soviet Union attempted to consolidate its power by using a method of compulsory forgetting known as a prison house of language, but the result was the production of many authors like Aleksandr Solzhenitsyn, Boris Pasternak, Mikhail Bulgakov, and Anatoly Rybakov. It is not so much that these authors' works constituted a direct resistance to power but rather that they constituted a form of recovery and treatment of a collective memory. Similarly, Czech author Milan Kundera's *The Book of Laughter and Forgetting* discusses the harm and deprivation that power had on his country, while the Hungarian author Ágota Kristóf's *Notebook* trilogy takes a people's darkest memories and drags them into the light. We could also cite countless other examples.

The situation in contemporary China, however, is completely different from thirty years ago, when, as in contemporary North Korea, all doors and windows to the outside world were tightly closed. In contemporary China, one window (the economy) is now open to the world while another (politics) remains closed, because of the state's need to control society and the people. This is where the problem lies. Related to the issue of memory and forgetting, the specificity of the current Chinese-style system of national amnesia can be found in the nation's half-open and half-closed windows.

First, under a powerful ideological system the partially open window is overseen by ideology. No one can directly observe the state's ideology, even as the state is constantly observing everything that every intellectual says, writes, or does. Furthermore, because this window can let in some sunlight, the world's wind and light have no choice but to surge in, thereby allowing people to experience enlightenment and the process of reform and opening up. The law does not have a specific significance with respect to memory and forgetting, and instead it exists in name only. It does not protect freedom of speech, freedom of the press, freedom to publish, or authors' freedom to imagine, nor does it protect people's freedom to remember or those people who are unwilling to forget. Instead, all hope rests with our leaders' enlightenment and morality.

Second, the partially open window has been opened not because of the efforts of intellectuals but rather because of power itself. Because the window has been opened as a result of the enlightenment and charity of certain figures, the people are therefore easily satisfied and display modest demands when it comes to the display of memory and amnesia. Therefore, once this window has been partially opened, people will no longer plead, summon, or struggle with power, attempting to return that other, unopened window to the people. After people who have long been locked in the dark are finally granted a window through which they can receive some sunlight and fresh air, how would they be able to demand that it be opened even wider? As a result, voluntary memories may pass through this half-open window, while compulsory amnesia remains locked behind the closed one. In contemporary China, this is the environment within which writers and intellectuals are willing to write—they express themselves within a space of voluntary memory while remaining silent within a space of compulsory amnesia. For China's intellectuals, the acceptance of amnesia constitutes a sort of collective compromise—a form of mutual understanding and tacit recognition following the abandonment of collective memories. These intellectuals feel that given that they still have air to breathe today, there is no need to make needless sacrifices for tomorrow. They remember what can be remembered and forget what must be forgotten. In this way they resemble obedient children who are awarded attention and candy for being well-behaved.

Third, intellectuals' tacit consent and approval of this amnesiac system derives from our country's current prosperity. Intellectuals who support this amnesia—be they authors or professors, historians or sociologists—see only what they are meant to see, and they don't look for anything else; they need only sing the praises of that which they are supposed to and not attempt to describe that which needs to be cast aside and forgotten; they need only apply their imagination to imagine what power, history, and reality demand and not permit the wings of their imagination to take them to regions that must be obscured and forgotten, or into the real sky. If intellectuals do this, they will be given power, honor, and money, but otherwise they will be silenced and even imprisoned (like Liu Xiaobo and all the philosophers, professors, and lawyers who have been designated as suspected provocateurs and arrested because they tried to commemorate June Fourth in the privacy of their own home). In contemporary China, money enjoys an incomparable strength and power, and is capable of sealing people's lips, drying up the ink in their pen, and making the wings of their literary imagination fly away from reality and conscience. Later, money uses art and the reputation of artists to grandly complete that magnificent reconstruction on the basis of the fictions and illusions resulting from the forgetting of history. In this way, reality is buried, conscience is castrated, and language is gang-raped by power and capital. Meanwhile, the time and history that are being artificially elevated by power are gradually helping complete this process of national forgetting, while at the same time creating a "new history." This new history then cultivates and nurtures everyone's habit of forgetting as well as their skepticism toward skepticism itself. Skeptics are always punished, while people who willingly believe lies and fictions, and who do not doubt that beneath the darkness there is a dazzling white background—they can all pocket their rewards.

As a result, this historical project of national amnesia has proven to be a great success.

The compulsory dimensions of this Chinese strategy of national amnesia have many parallels around the world, but its compromising and rewarding dimensions are unique to contemporary China. Thirty years ago, China used force to confront those who were unwilling to forget, but today this prosperous nation openly draws on its immense reserves of capital to use monetary rewards to help make people complicit in their own amnesia. Within literature and the arts, there is not a single national award in China that is sponsored by the people or by an independent organization. Instead, virtually all literature, arts, journalism, and culture prizes are administered by either the Party or the state, and consequently are complicit in this process of collective amnesia. This is not to say that the awards are completely worthless but rather that they permit you to write, create, and imagine only within a constrained area. As long as you remain within this constrained area, you will find success and will be rewarded with fame and accolades.

It must be admitted that the directors and deputy directors of the Chinese Writers' Association and China's Literary Federation, together with most of the directors of provincial-level, city-level, and even county-level and district-level writers' associations, include some of the most talented authors and artists in the nation or in their corresponding provinces, counties, or districts. Within the history, reality, and truth from which they are permitted to select, many authors use a combination of silence and selective speech, and within this area of compulsory amnesia and selective memory, they display their talented creativity and create a "good work" that is recognized by power, which invites those who have lost their memories to project a darkness within which it is impossible to see the truth, while inviting those who retain their memories to project a light and give accolades.

It is for this reason that these authors and artists become the directors and deputy directors of their corresponding writers' associations and literary federations. Their position represents not only a kind of power but also their achievement, glory, and symbolism in the path of artistic creation that they choose to pursue. Therefore, in choosing between memory and amnesia, talented and ambitious authors and artists often become complicit and silent. They remember what they need to remember and forget what they are told to forget—and in this way they help implement a process of selective memory. At most, they can wander along the margins of a history that needs to be suppressed and through the outskirts of a reality that needs to be forgotten. It is there that these authors and artists can collect some shards of memory, hit some harmless edge-balls, and win a few accolades that may help earn them some respect. In this way, even if an author or artist displays a sense of so-called conscience or valor, they simultaneously reflect the state's openness with respect to the fields of politics and the arts, together with a sense of enlightenment. In reality, the result is simply the uneasiness of compromise and symbolic displays of resistance, which is not the same as real freedom, conscience, and bravery. The outcome of this symbolic resistance to compulsory amnesia is that it permits power to make even greater use of the reputation of the arts to help implement and expand a national strategy of compulsory amnesia.

LITERATURE: RESISTING AMNESIA
AND EXTENDING MEMORY

Recently, the Swedish author and poet Kjell Erik Espmark's seven-volume novel *The Age of Amnesia* was published in Chinese translation. The work's first volume, titled *Amnesia*, describes the protagonist's loss of his memories—including his memories of love—and his subsequent attempts to recover them. This remarkable work explores the source of individual memory, as well as the frustrations involved in trying to recover one's memories when one finds oneself in an amnesiac state. Memory, in this novel, becomes a living entity and not merely an object or temporality. This differs from Chinese-style amnesia, where memory loss is a national process and is a result of the exercise of state power. What is forgotten are people's history and memories. Meanwhile, those who do forget are able to gain wealth, power, and prestige, and can even use their amnesia to obtain an enticing object of exchange from the state.

Amnesia focuses on individual memory loss, describing an individual's attempts to recover his former experiences, speech, and objects. Irrespective of what the author might have been thinking when he was writing this work, once the novel's translation was published in China, it was immediately viewed as an allegory of a process of national amnesia. That is to say, the work was read as a process of national amnesia projected onto a single individual. In losing our memories, what we lose first are our people's historical memories, followed by truth and reality. Eventually, every Chinese will come to resemble the novel's narrator, losing memories of his life, his loved ones, his loves and hatreds, and his joys and distresses. In this way, the part of your brain responsible for memory becomes completely blank, waiting for society, power, and others to tell you—based on their own needs—how you should understand your history, your society, and even your own past.

The state, power, and society want the intellectuals they oversee—including individuals in every region of the country, at every level of society, and in every environment—to resemble young children. They want to manage the country the way a preschool teacher looks after the children under his or her charge, such that everyone eats when they are supposed to eat and sleeps when they are supposed to sleep. And when these virtual children are supposed to play, they will lift a large red blossom with an innocent smile and add their own song or performance to a script someone else has already written. To achieve this objective, it will be necessary for everyone to lose their memories and also their ability to speak, such that the minds of the next generation will become a blank slate—an empty sheet of paper waiting to be written on. Afterward, the nation may come to resemble an enormous preschool—a wasteland to be reclaimed or a tract of virgin land to be cultivated. However, just as every preschool inevitably has some unruly children who do as they wish and not what their teacher tells them, a nation will similarly always have some authors and intellectuals who won't be willing to lose their memories and who will instead struggle to express themselves and allow the wings of their imagination to follow the path of soul, conscience, and art. They will struggle to flee the confined areas within which they are supposed to remain, and within any corner of history or reality, they will create works that contain memory.

Although memory is not the sole standard by which we may evaluate the worth of a work, it is certainly the most effective measure for evaluating whether a nation, party, or people is truly mature. Therefore, as an author I always retain a childlike fantasy—building on Ba Jin's dream— that one day it might be possible to erect a memorial in China to the Cultural Revolution. More than three decades have passed since the beginning of the Reform Era, and by now the nation should be mature and consummate, and should have enormous powers of forgiveness, introspection, and memory. Therefore, someone should not only create a memorial to the Cultural Revolution (today, no one even dares raise this possibility) but also erect a plaque in memory of the people's amnesia right in the middle of Tiananmen Square—the world's largest and most-visited square. Inscribed on this plaque there should be a record of all the traumas and memories our nation has suffered from mid-century onward, including the Anti-Rightist Campaign, the Great Leap Forward, the Three Years of Famine, the Cultural Revolution, and the student movement of 1989. A record of these national tragedies should be displayed in the most visible square in the world, informing everyone— Chinese and foreigners alike—that we Chinese are a mature, consummate people who dare to remember.

In this way, our nation would be truly great and respected, and would set an example for the world.

3 The Abjection of Alt-China and Its Literature

Standing before you here on such an elegant campus and at a university full of such outstanding scholars makes me feel as though I've entered another world. I'm reminded of two lines from China's great Eastern Jin poet Tao Yuanming from sixteen hundred years ago: "From the eastern hedge, I pluck chrysanthemum flowers / And idly look toward the southern hills," and "By mistake I sought mundane careers / And got entrapped in them for thirty years." I am also reminded of Tao Yuanming's Peach Blossom Spring fable about humanity's most beautiful utopia, of which we can truly say, "I don't know what year tonight is" and "I mistake this land for a strange land." At the same time, this campus also reminds me of Hong Kong—and specifically of the ocean, mountains, architecture, and learned teachers and students at the Hong Kong University of Science and Technology. For today's talk, accordingly, I'll begin with some reflections about Hong Kong.

At the beginning of this year, I found myself appointed as a visiting professor to teach creative writing at the Hong Kong University of Science and Technology. Because the scenery there is so beautiful, the teachers and students are so bright, and the classes are so relaxed, I'm able to enjoy a utopian life reminiscent of the Peach Blossom Spring. Reading, writing, teaching, and conversing—my life there is like a mid-spring day. One night this past May, I was deep in a beautiful dream when, at around 5:00 a.m., my bedside phone started ringing. The longer I delayed in answering it, the more insistently it rang. Eventually I couldn't stand it any longer and, with annoyance, I checked the number of the incoming call—it was my elder sister calling from our family's hometown in Henan, China. I picked up the phone and asked her what was wrong, and she replied that our mother had just had a dream in which I had committed a major mistake through my writing. In our mother's dream, I was afraid of being sent to prison, and therefore I knelt down and began kowtowing until my forehead was bloody and I was about to pass out. Upon waking up, Mother insisted that Elder Sister immediately call me to check and see how I was doing.

So Elder Sister asked, "Are you OK?"

I replied, "I'm fine. I'm doing very well."

She asked again, "Are you sure you're OK?"

I assured her, "Yes, I'm really OK. Everything is fine."

After confirming that I was OK, Elder Sister hung up.

This exchange reminded of the time I wrote an elementary-school composition about how my hometown had been the home of the Song Dynasty neo-Confucian philosophers Cheng Hao and Cheng Yi, known as the Cheng Brothers. However, some descendants of the Cheng Brothers felt that I was satirizing their illustrious ancestors rather than praising them, and therefore they summoned several other members of the Cheng clan to come teach a lesson to this "boy who likes to write." Afterward, my family and friends had to go to the homes of various members of the Cheng clan to offer gifts, apologize, and try to smooth things over. In this way, fortunately, the incident was resolved.

Later, I included a crippled character in one of my novels, but someone from my hometown read the work and assumed that this character was based on the village head's crippled son. The village head was quite displeased, and when I returned home for New Year's, my mother anxiously prepared some liquor and cigarettes and told me and my brother to take these gifts to the village head's home and apologize. I remember very clearly that on New Year's Eve, the village head was sitting on his bed and smoking a cigarette, while my brother and I stood in front of his bed and offered explanations and self-criticisms—insisting that the novel was all make-believe (which is to say, fiction) and had absolutely no connection to the villagers' real lives. Without looking at us or saying a word, the village head simply smoked, smoked, and smoked some more. The room was stifling, and I was afraid Elder Brother and I were going to pass out at any moment. Time became slow, heavy, and stagnant, as though it were already half-dead, to the point that every second seemed to drag on forever. Eventually, I promised the village head that I would never again include anything negative about our village in any of my novels, and only then did he finally stand up, put out his cigarette, and utter a simple yet powerful statement: "The two of you should leave now." With a deep sigh, as though we had just been pardoned, Elder Brother and I left the house.

After leaving the village head's enormous house, Elder Brother and I wandered through the countryside. On that New Year's Eve night, fireworks sounded nonstop in the streets, and Elder Brother let out another deep sigh, as though he had just been granted a new life. I, meanwhile, felt cold, solitary, and alone, as though the ocean had swallowed me up. From that point on, my writings seemed to be constantly hiding something. I was like a young child walking timidly down the road, afraid of snakes underfoot, eagles overhead, and wolves, dogs, and wild animals by the side of the road. It was the same way that the more you fear something on the road of life, the more frequently it will appear before you. I've always believed that the significance of my writings lay not in what I wrote but rather in what I *didn't* write—what I avoided and left out of my works. My whole life, it has always been precisely those times that I could not continue avoiding something, that I finally had no choice but to grab my pen and write. Therefore, I've often earnestly claimed that my art does not lie in my written works, but rather it lies outside of my works. Even so, I have continually been censored and banned, and to date I've had seven or eight works that could not be published or read in my own country. Meanwhile, those works that *could* be published invariably made my relatives, friends, and conscientious publishers feel very fearful and trepidatious. This situation initially persisted for a year or two, then for three or five years, and eventually for one, two, or even three decades. In the end, I've had this sort of experience for more than half my life, which is why, when my mother dreamed that I had incurred divine wrath on account of my writing and then kowtowed until my forehead was bloody, she therefore insisted that Elder Sister call me up in the middle of the night.

Elder Sister's phone call reminded me of a phrase: *abject literature.*

From that point on, the terms *abject* and *abject literature* have been permanently etched in my brain. Every day, every minute, and every second—

whenever I thought of literature, these terms would immediately spring to mind. Not only was I unable to make these terms disappear, but they also became clearer over time—like a nail embedded in a brick that becomes increasingly visible as the brick crumbles around it. Even now, as I stand before you, the terms *abject* and *abject literature* continue to resonate through my brain, like bees buzzing around a beehive or birds singing at dawn. I'm reminded of Japan's great novel *Tale of Genji* and China's own *Dream of the Red Chamber*, which share many similarities at the level of their writing and significance. Cao Xueqin, the author of *Dream of the Red Chamber*, once told his successors that because "I have no skills and my life is already half over," he therefore wanted to "compile a work that will bring joy to the world's people and shatter their sorrow." And although we don't know what precisely Murasaki Shikibu, the author of *Tale of Genji*, thought about her writing, from her novel we can infer that she, like Cao Xueqin, also wrote to bring joy to the world's people and shatter their sorrow. Compared to works by contemporary Chinese authors, we can see that Cao Xueqin's and Murasaki Shikibu's writings contain no trace of abjection or self-abasement, and instead their works possess an abundance of confidence in literature's dignity and sublimity.

As for contemporary Chinese authors, apart from the fact that none of us has the sort of talent that could be discussed in the same breath as that of Murasaki Shikibu and Cao Xueqin, which of us could share those earlier authors' sublime faith in the dignity of literature? Which of us would dare claim that we write to bring people joy and to shatter their sorrow? When literature faces reality and when authors confront power, who can avoid feeling the inherent abjection of authors and their literature? In contemporary China, authors are positioned so low that they risk becoming buried in the dust, but it is felt that if they were to be elevated, it would impede society's advancement and people's progress.

Today we are discussing a certain kind of literature, and the very possibility of that same literature. In a Chinese context, many people might view our approach as resembling ants worshipping moths as they fly into a flame, or the way the animals in George Orwell's *Animal Farm* sorrowfully long for the future. Moreover, the ideals, dreams, sublimity, and understanding of humanity that we find in contemporary Chinese literature—including qualities such as love, freedom, value, emotion, humanity, and the pursuit of soul—are inextricably entangled with issues of money, profit, nation, and power. These two sets of qualities cannot be disaggregated; consequently, in contemporary China there is a kind of author and literature that constantly appears out of place, and like weeds in a city's central park or thorn bushes in an urban forest, they are alienated to the point of being relegated to the wilderness at the outskirts of the city.

Regardless of whether Chinese literature can truly become integrated into world literature or will simply remain part of Asian literature, many authors continue to write feebly and abjectly, like lowly soy-sauce peddlers positioned at the margins of a flourishing society. In relation to the nation, this writing is comparable to a few weeds in a vast flower garden, but in artistic terms this kind of writing is the artist's very breath and existence. To tell the truth, I don't know whether the reality of contemporary China still needs our so-called literature, nor am I sure what the significance of this literature might be. This is like someone who continually faces the inevitability of death. Existence and meaninglessness, publication failures and writing frustrations, market and media manipulation, as well as literary policies, regulations, and restrictions—these factors all contribute to the abjection encountered by authors struggling to write in contemporary China. Because of this abjection, one *must write*, even as it is also precisely on account of this abjection that one can do nothing *other than write*. The result is a vicious cycle wherein authors write because of their abjection, even as their writing simultaneously renders them even more abject. The more they write, the more abject they become, and the more abject they become, the more they write. This is like Don Quixote battling the windmills, and although it might appear as though the windmills were created for Don Quixote, it is also true that Don Quixote was himself created for the windmills. But what does this mean? What is the significance of this symbiotic relationship between Don Quixote and the windmills?

Could it be that all of this is meaningless?

I remember how when I started to write *Dream of Ding Village* and *Ballad, Hymn, Ode* more than a decade ago, I underwent a rigorous process of self-criticism. When I now look back at the process of writing and publishing those novels, however, I wonder how much literary life they actually contain?

In Europe, America, Japan, South Korea, and most of the world's other countries and territories (though not North Korea), many readers, scholars, experts, and media workers often focus on China's censorship regime and its restrictions on freedom of speech, and therefore view Chinese authors as global orphans for whom they feel pity, sympathy, and sorrow. I am grateful that our international colleagues have taken such an interest in Chinese literature. To you, I say, thank you, thank you, thank you!

At the same time, although for Chinese authors censorship is a kind of prison they must strive to reject, we must also ask why is it that Russian and former Soviet authors, even when facing the White Terror or the possibility of execution or exile to Siberia, were able to create literary masterpieces such as *The Gulag Archipelago*, *Doctor Zhivago*, *The Master and Margarita*, and *Life and Fate* yet Chinese authors have suffered similar hardships but have not produced these sorts of masterpieces?

Although Chinese literature is still operating under a rigorous censorship system, the current literary and social environment is a far cry from that of the Cultural Revolution or the Anti-Rightist Campaign, much less the former Soviet Union's White Terror or its Siberia exile camps. Nevertheless, China still has not produced an Aleksandr Solzhenitsyn, Boris Pasternak, Mikhail Bulgakov, Anatoly Rybakov, or Vasily Grossman. And if one feels that earlier Chinese authors were so enmeshed in politics that their artistic creation became a new form of bondage, then why hasn't contemporary China—with its 1.3 billion people and its several thousand years of cultural heritage—been able to produce a Leo Tolstoy, Fyodor Dostoevsky, or Anton Chekhov? Why hasn't it been able to produce a Franz Kafka, James Joyce, Marcel Proust, Samuel Beckett, Albert Camus, Vladimir Nabokov, Gabriel García Márquez, or Jorge Luis Borges, or a Mori Ōgai, Natsume Sōseki, Ryūnosuke Akutagawa, Yasunari Kawabata, or Yukio Mishima? Why is it that today we don't even have writers comparable to early twentieth-century Chinese authors like Lu Xun, Xiao Hong, Shen Congwen, and Eileen Chang?

Of course, every era is different and must have its own authors and literary works. However, contemporary China's era and reality, its history and current possibilities, are obvious to viewers around the world. Its richness and variety, strangeness and vigor, the complexity of human emotion and the absurdity of world affairs, constantly changing yet ever stable, from system to contemporary reality, from contemporary reality to history, and from society to human emotion—I believe this is all a wondrous thing that the twentieth century has handed down to the twenty-first.

Strangers in a strange land.

If you were to ask me to reflect on contemporary China from the perspective of pure literature, and to assess the nation and its people without relying on any political or moral standards, I might offer the following three theses:

1 Contemporary China is the most unique nation in the world.
2 Contemporary China's era is the most unique era in world history.
3 Contemporary China has the most distinctive "Chinese-style people" in the world.

There is a concept under which there exist two realities. This concept is that of a strange or "alt-"China, and the two realities are those of an alt-era and an alt-people—in other words, alt-China's era and its people. And what about the corresponding literature? To tell the truth, Chinese authors have yet to write a Chinese-style novel addressing this alt-China. We do not yet have a Chinese literature that would match this nation and its history, contemporary reality, and its "Chinese-style people."

In this alt-China and its 1.3 billion people, the stories that unfold daily are enough to fill the pages of a hundred almost unimaginably great masterpieces. However, day after day, year after year, and decade after decade, we have consistently failed to produce a work capable of living up to the distinctiveness of this alt-China—a great work like *War and Peace, Crime and Punishment, Ulysses, Remembrance of Things Past, The Castle, One Hundred Years of Solitude, The Makioka Sisters, The Old Capital, The True Story of Ah Q, Border Town,* or *Tales of Hulan River.* That is to say, in contemporary China there are countless stories that belong to humanity but don't belong to any other nation, nationality, or language, just as there are countless fictional characters who belong to world literature but don't belong to any other language, culture, nationality, or nation. Nevertheless, we still have not yet managed to write a truly "Chinese story" that could belong to world literature and to humanity while at the same time capturing the distinctiveness of alt-China's Chinese story and Chinese people.

From a literary perspective, alt-China—which is to say, today's China—is no longer the China of Lu Xun's era, nor is it the China of the post-1949 Mao Zedong era or of Deng Xiaoping's Reform and Opening Up era. For contemporary authors, the nation's transformations, complexity, and absurdity contain far too many deep and complex Chinese stories, not to mention a diversity of fictional characters who fall under the category of Chinese humanity. However, when Chinese literature encounters this alt-China and its alt-era, the literature lacks a great story or fictional character that we might recognize as being quintessentially Chinese.

Why is this the case? I think the reason can be reduced to the following factors:

1 To a greater or lesser extent, all world literatures begin to deteriorate through the process of cultural creation, and Chinese literature is no exception.
2 China currently finds itself in a distorted, deformed, and irregular new era. This is an era of money, power, the market, and new media, and it marks the birth of the great new Chinese literature and fictional characters that we have been discussing, thereby creating an unprecedented level of temptation and oppression.
3 It certainly cannot be denied that Chinese literature lacks a free and relaxed imagination and a social environment for creation.

These three sets of factors have created a bottleneck that is currently impeding contemporary Chinese literature's development. However, what I want to emphasize here is that although Chinese authors' works encounter countless obstacles, bottlenecks, and impossibilities in the contemporary era, it must nevertheless be acknowledged that, when it comes to creative resources, we currently find ourselves in the best era of the past century, and when it comes to writing environment, we have reached the most favorable period of the past half century. Why, then, is it that, during this alt-Chinese era—in which the writing environment is relatively relaxed and writing resources are abundant—we have not been able to produce the sorts of distinctively Chinese works that could rank among the world's best? Today's Chinese nation and Chinese people have established themselves as among the world's most unique, so why have we not been able to create similarly uniquely Chinese stories and characters in our literature? Why have we not managed to create a distinctively Chinese literature?

Apart from the constraints placed on authors by tradition, culture, reality, censorship, and national conditions, I would also like to stress the authors' own awareness of—and adaptation to—the censorship system, wherein the authors engage in a process of reflexive self-censorship that follows the external censorship process. The result is that after working for years under this censorship system, authors may gradually lose their ability to grasp people, reality, history, and their contemporary era. This, in other words, is the abjection with which Chinese literature approaches contemporary reality, together with its reflexive acceptance of that abjection. It is a fact that authors find themselves in an era of abject literature and are rarely able to truly awaken from the resulting state of abjection. This resembles the way that as an ant (an author) clings to life after having been run over by a car (reality), it still believes in its own future, or the way that after a sparrow flies from one part of the sky to another, it believes it owns the entire sky, including even the portions that extend over the endless oceans and the polar regions. When facing the Earth, the ant is unaware that it has just been crushed and therefore has no sense of abjection, just as, when facing the sky, the sparrow is unaware of its own miniscule size and therefore has no sense of abjection either. Meanwhile, when Chinese literature faces the grotesqueness, complexity, richness, and uniqueness of contemporary China and its people, it loses the ability to master that reality and becomes complacent. As a result, it no longer has the same sense of abjection when facing alt-China and its alt-era.

There is no longer that sense of abjection that authors and literature encounter in real life.

Despite finding itself in this Chinese era with its unique people, Chinese literature does not feel at all abject on account of not having managed to produce a Chinese story that would be unique within world literature—the way Lu Xun produced the paradigmatically Chinese character Ah Q. Chinese literature currently finds itself in an abject era of an alt-China from which many authors like myself have not yet managed to awaken. When it comes to writing, however, I'm not certain this is necessarily a bad thing. Perhaps Chinese authors, precisely because they have not yet awakened, will be able to tell a great Chinese story—the same way that Shakespeare was able to write his great works precisely because he did not know that he was going to be great. On the other hand, Shakespeare's talent was an outlier among outliers, and countless other great authors were able to produce their great works only through a process of fully conscious hard work.

To return to my own writing practice—including my novels *The Four Books* and *The Explosion Chronicles*, although neither of them is particularly worth mentioning here—over nearly a decade of writing, I've come to appreciate an author's fundamental inability to grasp alt-China's history, its contemporary reality, and its unique people. I've come to appreciate that this series of writings and publications, readings and critiques, contributes to the feeling of helpless abjection that an author feels when faced with alt-China's most distinctively Chinese story and Chinese people. This feeling of helpless abjection yields the sort of endless chain of confrontation and compromise that we observe in Don Quixote's battles with the windmills. In the end, it is not that the author fails to discern and master alt-China's distinctively Chinese story and Chinese characters, the same way that it was not the windmills that defeated Don Quixote, but rather that the author and Don Quixote both were unable to master their own lives. The problem is that the Chinese author, when faced with alt-China's distinctively Chinese story and Chinese people, comes to doubt the life and artistic value of his own works.

Given that in Spain the wind can blow endlessly and windmills can spin forever, if Don Quixote were still alive, how could he not have already exhausted himself and acknowledged defeat? In the face of infinite time, life resembles leaves in the autumn wind and the winter chill, while art resembles someone facing the beauty of a cemetery. Therefore, when I receive people's questions here and throughout the world, I always respond with a smile and say honestly, "China is currently in a much better position than before. It really is. Thirty years ago, if, for the sake of literature or art, you wrote something that 'wasn't permitted,' you might be separated from your family, imprisoned, or even executed. Today, however, am I not perfectly all right as I stand before you here? Am I not still able to lecture and travel, chat and dine with you, and even discuss literature and art with you? At the same time, however, I must always emphasize that if a subset of Chinese authors like myself face alt-China's writing dilemmas, it is not merely for the sake of compromise that we let art yield to the state, the collective, reality, power, and censorship. More importantly, it is that we ourselves, in alt-China and its alt-era, overlook this enormous and powerful condition of 'alt-'—the enormous differences that mark alt-China, its alt-era, and the Chinese people in contemporary Chinese-styled humanity. To put this simply, the primary reason why we are unable to write great masterpieces lies with ourselves. It is a result of the fact that we have not acknowledged the startling abjection with which literature faces this vast alt-China and its alt-era, and our authors have not truly awakened from alt-China's abjection."

But have you not awakened from that state of abjection?

Do I not recognize the abject attitude with which literature regards alt-China?

Yes, I did recognize literature's startling abjection within this alt-China and its alt-era. However, this recognition became clear only in my recent writings. To tell the truth, it was only after I received Elder Sister's phone call earlier this year that this finally became clear to me. You could even say that it was only in giving this lecture that literature's abjection within alt-China finally became clear to me. Looking back at the difficulties I encountered in writing and publishing *The Four Books* and *The Explosion Chronicles*, I have no desire to resent, criticize, or complain. Compared to earlier generations of Chinese authors, I am content to be able to continue writing and am gratified to be able to write what I want. This is because I know very well that this is literature's understanding and recognition of abjection. More importantly, I am finally beginning to actively lay claim to literature's abjection in alt-China. I hope that through a self-conscious act of claiming, I'll be able to attain some insight into and rescue from abjection. I also hope that by being rescued from abjection, I will also be able to rescue and support my own writing. Here, literature's abjection is not only a function of the existence of a kind of alt-China; it is also an even more different kind of art and force, which is the eternal life of the author and of literature itself.

I've recently begun to realize that in today's China—in this alt-China and its alt-era—there is a need for authors who write because of and for this abjection. The more abject everything becomes, the more these authors should write; and the more they write, the more abject everything will become. This is how things are—literature exists because of abjection, while abjection awaits literature's art. As for me, I've finally become a self-claimant on behalf of alt-China's abjection! From now on, abjection will be the entirety of my literature, as well as the entirety of my life. All my future writings will be born from abjection and will exist on account of abjection. Without abjection, my (our) future literature would not exist. Without abjection, the past, present, and future author known as Yan Lianke would not exist. For him, abjection is not only a kind of life but also a form of literary eternity. It is the entirety of his future life, literature, and art.

At this point I am reminded of *One Thousand and One Nights*. In that work's famous story of the wooden horse, the horse was originally made from ebony wood, but if you pressed a tiny peg behind its ear, it would fly off into the sky. I wonder whether in relation to my literature, abjection might perhaps resemble that tiny peg? Perhaps my literature might, thanks to a tiny peg, become an ebony horse able to take me anywhere? I think that, with respect to my future writings, when I no longer have an abject existence and after my abjection is stripped from me, then that wooden horse might die, after which it wouldn't be able to travel anywhere at all. I am therefore grateful for the abjection of alt-China's literature. I am grateful for the existence of this abjection and for the fact that it permits me to write. I am also grateful for the fact that because I write, I am able to further nurture alt-China's and its alt-era's vast abject abjection that exists within the author's heart. Here, the abject abjection transcends life, writing, publishing, reading, and especially the restrictions on power and regulations, and the author's existence, while also becoming an individual life within alt-China and its alt-era—becoming an author writing within a condition of "alt-" itself. This abject abjection within a condition of "alt-" appears to have been with me since birth, and it will remain with me to the end. For that reason, I am also reminded of a palace in a faraway country to which that divine horse would be able to fly.

One day, the emperor took a poet (an author) to visit his labyrinthine palace. Upon seeing the majestic palace, the poet was silent for a moment; then he recited a short poem. Contained within this short poem was the palace's entire structure, architecture, furnishings, and landscaping. The emperor exclaimed, "Poet, you've stolen my palace!" whereupon the executioner lowered his blade and ended the poet's life. In this "Fable of the Palace," the life of the poet or author is snuffed out. But is this a tragedy? No, not at all! It is an elegy, memorializing the poet's artistry and power, and his talent, which was as magnificent as the palace itself. And what about us? We won't speak of a short poem—even with a long poem, a long prose piece, an epically long creation, how could we manage to include the entire palace together with even a portion of the tiles and flowers inside the palace?

We do not die because one of our poems can contain an entire palace but rather because a hundred of our poems are still inferior to a single tile or flower belonging to this alt-era's palace—this is our contemporary abjection. It is the result of literature's abjection, and that abjection's harvest. Therefore, it is for the sake of the alt-era's abjection that we live and write. And, in the future, it will be for the sake of the alt-era's abjection that we will die. Today, I stand here before you, on this solemn occasion, to discuss literature with friends, teachers, experts, and fellow authors—to discuss literature's abjection in alt-China and its alt-era. This is precisely so that I and other authors like me can emerge from contemporary China's "Peach Blossom Spring" and truly enter alt-China and its alt-era. It is so that we may emerge from alt-China's historical utopia and that never again shall we "from the eastern hedge, pluck chrysanthemum flowers / And idly look toward the southern hills," and never again shall we remark that "I don't know what year tonight is" or "I mistake this land for a strange land."

We want to treat art's strength as strength, and treat everyone's collective love for people, literature, the world, and humanity as literature's only resource. We want to comfort abjection and offer it life's power, vision, and future, so that abjection may continue to exist, so that it may exist independently in the palace of alt-China and its alt-era, and so that, smiling, it may freely depart through the main entrance of the alt-era's palace. We want poets to be able to live not only in the palace but also outside the palace so that they can live not only in this boundary zone but also outside it. In this way, their writing may be able to transcend power, transcend the nation, transcend all borders, and ultimately return to literature's own life, humanity, and soul. We not only want poets and authors to continue to live and chant; we also want them to believe that abjection is this alt-era's existence, life, and reality, as well as a kind of true ideal, force, and everlasting art. This is art's eternity and future, and it is the reason why art can be great and eternal. Accordingly, we want authors in alt-China and its alt-era to recognize abjection, accept abjection, and endure abjection. Moreover, we want them to write lengthily and eternally because of abjection, and for abjection.

4 The Wild Child That Is American Literature

America—the impression most Chinese have of America is that although the nation may not be very reasonable, it is certainly quite powerful. And because America is so powerful, it often focuses on its own interests without attending to anyone else's. In this respect, America is like a rebellious teen—it cannot stop stirring up trouble around the world, although it also has a firm sense of justice, chivalry, and even righteousness. Whenever it encounters an injustice, it immediately rushes over to lend a hand, but when it encounters adversaries whom it perceives to be weak and unreasonable, it doesn't hesitate to squash them like a bug.

In short, this child is a lot of fun but is also a bit wild.

This is the impression many Chinese writers have of twentieth-century American literature—or at least it's *my* impression. I feel that American literature is like America itself, and given that Americans have had such a short history, their traditional culture appears immature and even slightly ridiculous—like a young child discussing his or her former lives. In the streets of New York, aside from reinforced concrete structures and advertisements, exhibits and shops devoted to modernist art, there are also lots of people and cars (though far fewer than in contemporary Beijing). In New York, San Francisco, Seattle, or even here in Austin, Texas, you won't find a single stone from Egypt or ancient Greece, or a single brick from London, Paris, or any other European city, nor will you find a single grain of yellow earth or drop of water from Asia. Instead, it is what it is—an adolescent, heedless of other people and other things.

American literature is also like this. The compassionate sorrow one sees in Russian literature is nowhere to be found in American literature. The careful and cautious exploration that one observes in European literature is replaced, in American literature, with something that is simply stated directly. This becomes a literary eruption that makes the powerful shout out in delight and the oppressed moan in agony. The result is that America's literature, particularly in the twentieth century, carries a youthful rhythm even in moments of ecstasy—reverberating not only throughout modern America but also throughout the ancient Chinese continent.

THE AMERICAN WIND BLOWING IN FROM THE CHINESE LITERARY SCENE

When I compare American literature to a wild child, I am primarily referring to the impression of American literature that I developed in the 1980s and 1990s. At that time, China had just awakened from the decade-long nightmare that was the Cultural Revolution, and the society was riddled with a thousand wounds while its economy was laced with a thousand fissures. People had very conservative opinions, and they also viewed Western civilization and America's modern culture with a combination of curiosity and apprehension. The Chinese people were like a contemporary North Korean who is suddenly deposited in the streets of a European or American city and exclaims, "Oh, so this is what the world is like! This is what literature is all about!" At that point, Chinese authors had long been imprisoned within the cage of Soviet-style socialist realist revolutionary literature (from which even today they have not truly freed themselves), and they regarded Maxim Gorky as a literary idol.

It was at this point that there was the literary equivalent of a cock greeting a new dawn, as great works from around the world began pouring into Chinese bookstores and became accessible to Chinese readers. The Chinese revered nineteenth-century Russian literature and French, English, and German classics as they might revere old, white-haired scholars. Twentieth-century Latin American literature had a natural connection with Chinese rural culture and was therefore enthusiastically embraced, and even though Chinese authors and readers were not able to fully understand European literature's stream of consciousness or the

French *nouvelle roman*, they nevertheless found them easy to praise. It was as though we had been given a name-brand suit and, despite finding it extremely uncomfortable and unattractive, we still wore it—simply because it was a famous name brand. This imported literature was similarly a prominent name brand that we didn't dare reject. For instance, Chinese authors were astounded by French absurdist dramas such as *Waiting for Godot* and *The Bald Soprano*. In fact, although to this day Samuel Beckett's and Eugène Ionesco's plays have never been performed in China and are seldom even read, as soon as Chinese authors hear their names, they immediately begin discussing the playwrights' lives and works with great familiarity. This is truly an adorable phenomenon, as though everyone were very familiar with God despite never having encountered Him or even read the Bible.

American literature, however, is a different matter altogether. During contemporary Chinese literature's golden age in the 1980s and 1990s, no country or region in the world had as much influence on Chinese authors and readers as the United States. In terms of sheer numbers of authors introduced into China, even if you were to add up the authors from all over Europe, they still wouldn't match those from the United States. Latin American literature has also been very influential in China, but if you add up all the Latin American authors who have been introduced into China, you'll find that the total is significantly fewer than the number of authors from the United States. For Chinese readers, nineteenth-century authors like Mark Twain and Jack London appeared somewhat old-fashioned, although Mark Twain's humor offered a stark contrast to contemporary China and demonstrated to Chinese authors that humor could be deployed as a legitimate art form. Similarly, although Jack London's novels are wild and unbridled, Chinese readers found in them the possibility of writing about cruelty, survival, humanity, and greed, to the point that you could strip your characters down to a state of utter nakedness. In this way, Chinese authors learned that rather than simply describing fictional characters, it was possible to extract their inner soul and lay it out it in front of the reader.

The Beat Generation sought to write about a decadent vitality— describing the utter rot and decay of life itself, combined with the stench and texture of flesh and bones decaying in a putrid ditch. Whether they were smoking, doing drugs, eating, or having sex, their speech and behavior appear as natural as windswept leaves and rain. Jack Kerouac, Allen Ginsberg, and William Burroughs—and particularly works like *On the Road, The Town and the City, Howl, Junkie,* and *Naked Lunch*—swept through China like a tornado and were influential not only for their textual meaning but also for their spiritual significance. It was not so much that Chinese readers accepted these works as great literature but rather that they accepted them as teachings of spiritual freedom. These works taught Chinese authors and readers that one can ignore or even resist revolution, and that it was possible for them to follow their authentic self, rather than adhering to a stale sense of sublimity. Because these works were so influential, subsequent ones like Neal Cassady's *The First Third,* Joyce Johnson's *Minor Characters,* John Clellon Holmes's *Go,* and Chandler Brossard's *Who Walk in Darkness* followed like clouds of dust swept up by this literary tornado and were similarly embraced by Chinese readers.

Although America's Lost Generation doesn't boast as many authors and works as the Beats, the term *lost generation* nevertheless caught hold within Chinese literary circles. In the 1980s the Chinese people woke up as if from a long dream—finding themselves sleepy and confused, uncertain where their society was heading. At the time, China's politics, culture, and literature were full of aspiration and confusion. Young people were not sure what they should do, yet they idealistically continued trying to enact change. *Lost generation* captured this Chinese generation's plight, deftly describing its mood and condition. Now, three decades later, the members of the Chinese Lost Generation are already middle-aged or even older, although they are followed by their younger brothers and sisters, together with the children who were born in that same era. Meanwhile, contemporary China's post-1980s and post-1990s generations spend every day scurrying around trying to secure a career, a salary, a house, and a car, and therefore could similarly be viewed as a sort of lost generation.

Originally, the Lost Generation didn't offer Chinese readers many literary works that could compare to Beat Generation classics like *On the Road*, *Howl*, and *Naked Lunch*. Instead, the Lost Generation's works were darker and possessed a greater poetic sentimentality and sense of disillusionment. The Beat authors were simple, absolute, and incorrigible, whereas the Lost Generation authors were romantic and poetic, capable of falling down but also of getting back up. In contemporary China, accordingly, the Beat Generation's legacy lies primarily in its works and activities, whereas the Lost Generation persists as an ideal, a banner, and even an ideology.

Among the Lost Generation authors, Ernest Hemingway is virtually the only one who has been fully embraced in China. In a broader sense, however, the impression people have of Hemingway is primarily a result of works like *The Old Man and the Sea* and *For Whom the Bell Tolls*, together with his legendary biography and his receipt of the Nobel Prize, and people have less awareness of his connection to the Lost Generation.

"Black Humor" refers to a movement that remains popular and influential in China to this day. This was one of the genres that was introduced three decades ago, when American authors and literary works first began appearing on the Chinese literary scene. Readers and critics responded to Joseph Heller's *Catch-22* like a well-bred young man or woman who suddenly realizes that masturbation carries no physical consequences. If they realize that it is acceptable to speak about their fondness for masturbation, however, would this not be equivalent to peeling off a scab and reopening a bloody wound? Black Humor takes the amusement and humor traditionally associated with entertainment, fun, and health, and instead grounds them on sorrow, helplessness, and absurdity. Even today, thirty years after its initial publication, *Catch-22* remains on Chinese bookshelves, claiming a space in the hearts of China's rebellious and creative authors. Along with works like Kurt Vonnegut's *Breakfast of Champions* and *Slaughterhouse-Five* and Thomas Pynchon's *V* and *Gravity's Rainbow*, Heller's *Catch-22* has become an essential topic whenever Chinese authors discuss American literature. The only unfortunate thing is that although Pynchon was introduced into China along with Heller and Vonnegut, at the time his works had not yet been translated into Chinese, so readers did not appreciate him as much as they did those other two authors.

Literature needs opportunities. If you arrive at an opportune moment, you may become a household name and become canonized, but if you are even just a bit late, you might still achieve a canonical status but won't necessarily become a household name. In this respect, Heller and Vonnegut were successes, whereas Pynchon was a relative failure. Other works associated with the Black Humor movement included William Gaddis's *The Recognitions*, Thomas Berger's *Little Big Man*, and John Hawkes's *The Blood Oranges*. Because these latter authors couldn't keep up with the three-wheeled cart that was Heller, Vonnegut, and Pynchon, however, they arrived late in China and could only become green leaves surrounding Black Humor's "bloody blossom."

For many reasons, China has long been obsessed with the Nobel Prize. Countries like the United States and France win Nobel Prizes like bright children awarded little red blossoms after turning in their homework. After Sinclair Lewis became the first American to be awarded a Nobel Prize in Literature, in 1930, Eugene O'Neill won it six years later, followed in 1938 by Pearl Buck, who is very familiar to Chinese readers, and by William Faulkner in 1949. In 1954 Hemingway finally got his wish, overcoming his disappointment that Faulkner had been awarded the prize before him. The prize was awarded to John Steinbeck in 1962, to Saul Bellow in 1976, and to Isaac Bashevis Singer in 1978. Fifteen years later, Toni Morrison became the first African American to win the prize.

Although the United States hasn't won a Nobel Prize in Literature in the past twenty years, from China's perspective Americans have already won this prize too many times. It is as though you view the prize as your family's apple tree, from which you can reach out and pick a fruit whenever you wish. Over the past century, American authors have won the prize nine times, averaging once per decade. Compared to China, with its 3,000-year history and its 1.4 billion people, you have certainly received more than your share. You already had nine of these prizes while we didn't receive a single one during the entire first century of the prize's existence. And here I will add that, for reasons that everyone already knows, the Chinese don't regard Gao Xingjian as one of their own; consequently, they were not at all excited when he won the prize in 2000 (at the time I gave this lecture, Mo Yan had not yet been awarded the prize; when he received the prize six months later, the Chinese people were of course delighted).

China's love and reverence for the Nobel Prize was as though the Chinese people, although disappointed that their soccer team was not playing well, eventually came to love the game even more. You Americans simply cannot comprehend the Chinese fascination with the Nobel Prize. Therefore, when American laureates and their works are introduced into China, they do not merely ride the wave but rather shine brightly in all directions. Of the nine American laureates listed above, Pearl Buck was already well known in China because she wrote about Chinese topics, whereas the others achieved recognition on account of their works combined with the fame that these authors accrued from winning the prize. The American laureates who are most often read and cited by Chinese include Faulkner, Hemingway, Bellow, Singer, and Morrison, particularly the first three, although in Chinese theatrical circles O'Neill enjoys a reputation and stature comparable to that which Faulkner enjoys within fictional circles.

Thirty years ago, China's literary scene and its reading community were enthralled by works like Hemingway's "The Snows of Kilimanjaro," *The Old Man and the Sea*, *For Whom the Bell Tolls*, *A Farewell to Arms*, and *The Sun Also Rises*; Faulkner's *The Sound and the Fury*, *As I Lay Dying*, *Light in August*, and *Absalom, Absalom!*; Bellow's *Humboldt's Gift*, *Herzog*, and *Henderson the Rain King*; and O'Neill's *Beyond the Horizon*, *Long Day's Journey into Night*, and *Desire under the Elms*; together with Steinbeck's *Grapes of Wrath*, Singer's *The Magician of Lublin*, and Morrison's *Song of Solomon*. To this day, the intoxicating aroma of that spring breeze can still be smelled by Chinese readers, who then go off in search of these authors and their works. These authors helped American literature earn a reputation in China comparable to that which God earned for his teachings, and to this day people in China would probably find it inconceivable that you might want to write fiction without knowing your Faulkner and Hemingway, and without having read *The Old Man and the Sea*, *The Sound and the Fury*, and *As I Lay Dying*.

The United States has many other authors and literary works that have been embraced in China irrespective of their literary school and without

Chinese readers even knowing how the works are classified in the United States. As Western winds blew into the country, many authors benefited from this situation. Rather than relying on the reputation of their respective literary schools, they instead relied on their works' individual character, beauty, and magic, and after marching into China they quickly became fashionable, conquering everything in their path. They managed to win over virtually all Chinese readers who still retained a fondness for literature, such that their works came to influence not only this contemporary generation of authors and readers but also ones that followed.

When J. D. Salinger's *The Catcher in the Rye* first entered China thirty years ago, the work's influence was initially rather limited, although later it spread like a tornado—resembling the now-ubiquitous McDonald's and KFC franchises that have sprouted up throughout the country. In fact, it reached the point that wherever you went, you wouldn't be able to find anyone who had not read—or at least heard of—Salinger's novel, the same way that there isn't a single child currently living in Chinese urban areas who has never eaten at McDonald's or KFC.

Meanwhile, Vladimir Nabokov's *Lolita* and Henry Miller's *Tropic of Cancer* didn't appear on China's literary scene until a little later. When *Lolita* first appeared in Chinese bookstores and street stalls, it was examined with a curious and moralistic gaze by a nation that, until very recently, had been insular and constrained. Afterward, Chinese readers began to approach the work the same way they had secretly discussed British author D. H. Lawrence's *Lady Chatterley's Lover*, and although they understood Nabokov's novel at a technical level, they were also deeply confused by it. It would not be until several years later that Nabokov would begin to be recognized in China as the most significant author writing in the English language.

When *Tropic of Cancer* was introduced into China in the early 1990s, its reception differed from that of *Lolita* in a subtle yet important respect. In China there had long been a veil of fascinated silence surrounding the topic of sex. On one hand, there was a saying that material comforts lead to lewd desires, but on the other hand, sex had long been perceived as a source of trouble, which is why *Lolita* was initially not regarded as a work of serious literature. After having endured a lengthy period of political oppression, however, Chinese readers were far more fascinated with banned books than they were with any of the world's prestigious literary prizes, which is why they felt such reverence for former Soviet authors Aleksandr Solzhenitsyn and Boris Pasternak, and Czech author Milan Kundera. Chinese readers regarded these latter figures as their respective nations' conscience. Even after *Tropic of Cancer* was banned in the United States, it continued to be secretly read by American soldiers on the front during World War II, and it was said that these soldiers often described scenes from the novel when they sent letters home. When Miller's work arrived in China, it was perceived as much more mysterious and sublime than Nabokov's.

It was therefore not important whether Nabokov and Miller technically belonged to the category of Black Humor. The fate of their works and of the authors themselves, together with the mystery of their stories, had already transcended narrow considerations of literary taxonomy. Nabokov's and Miller's sense of independence, combined with their determination to write as they wished and irrespective of what others might say about them, had long since transcended the question of which literary school they might technically belong to. There were also some authors, such as F. Scott Fitzgerald and John Updike, who weren't introduced into China until much later and who were never fully embraced by Chinese readers. For instance, from the very beginning *The Great Gatsby* was recognized as a canonical work, although Chinese readers remained somewhat distant from it. The entry of Updike's Rabbit trilogy into China coincided with the nation's period of cultural fever, and unfortunately at that time Chinese readers were far more interested in literature that was innovative and unusual as opposed to literature that was realistic and traditional. Later, the Japanese author Haruki Murakami was so fascinated by American authors such as Truman Capote and the so-called minimalist author Raymond Carver that he introduced countless Chinese readers to Carver's short stories and to Capote's novels like *Breakfast at Tiffany's* and *In Cold Blood*. Unlike earlier American authors, who were like a breath of fresh air when they were introduced into China, these latter works resembled mere tributaries of a larger river.

As for contemporary authors like Philip Roth and Paul Auster, who have both had several works translated into Chinese, their reception simply cannot be compared to that of authors who were introduced before them. This has nothing to do with their works themselves, but rather it is a result of the fact that their writing style deviated from what Chinese readers had come to expect from American literature, not to mention the fact that today's China is no longer a country that holds culture, literature, and reading in high esteem.

AMERICAN LITERATURE'S WILD-CHILD IMAGE

There is no question that American literature is rich and complicated and that any attempt to reduce it to a specific appearance will inevitably result in an oversimplification. I have read only the equivalent of a single drop of this vast sea of American literature—including the innovation of James Fenimore Cooper's *The Pioneers*, the historical quality of Harriet Beecher Stowe's *Uncle Tom's Cabin*, the romanticism and social critique of Nathaniel Hawthorne's *The Scarlet Letter*, the broad lyricism of Theodore Dreiser's *Sister Carrie*, the allegory and symbolism of Herman Melville's *Moby-Dick*, and, of course, O. Henry's famous twist endings. However, when the modern American novel entered its post–World War II golden age, there was a proliferation of literary movements and a swarm of authors following the expansion of the United States' politics, economy, and culture.

It was at this point that the form of this literary wild child finally began to take shape. Because the Lost Generation was lost, it hesitated, and because it hesitated, it became wild. For Chinese readers this, combined with Hemingway's notorious lack of restraint and his personal stubbornness, marked the point at which the perception of American literature as a wild child began to emerge. This process continued with the stories, narratives, and characters associated with the Beat Generation, not to mention the behavior of the authors themselves—which included the way their naked spirits attempted to break through all social constraints, their insistence on doing things their own way, their sense of freedom and independence, their unconventionality, their hedonism, and the way their quest for freedom led them to explode in a burst of flame.

Black Humor authors such as Heller, Vonnegut, and Pynchon, together with affiliated authors such as Nabokov and Miller, each had their own distinctive writing style, although collectively they shared certain characteristics. Yet it must also be admitted that their most iconic works—including *Catch-22*, *Breakfast of Champions*, *Slaughterhouse-Five*, *Gravity's Rainbow*, *V*, *Lolita*, *Tropic of Cancer*, and *Tropic of Capricorn*—

were all paradigmatically representative of their people and their era, of the contradictions that characterized its environment, and of the tendency of people in this sort of environment to overturn all existing conventions and pursue their own freedom. Even a gentle novel like *The Catcher in the Rye* reflects an aversion and resistance to heroes and a sense of order, and it was precisely this underlying attitude that helped Salinger's relatively simple work attain worldwide recognition. This was especially true in China, where readers liked the novel not because it was by a twentieth-century author, or because of the care Salinger took with revising his manuscript, or because of the nutritious sustenance that he provided for future generations of authors, but rather because of the nonconformist and rebellious tendencies of Salinger's protagonist, Holden Caulfield.

Many Chinese readers are uncertain whether *The Catcher in the Rye* should be viewed as a work of elite literature or merely pulp fiction. If they view it as the former, it is because Salinger uses such a lyrical and poetic style to present his characters and his story, which expresses the resistance and freedom that many Chinese desire. If they view it as the latter, it is because it is difficult to find much in the text in the way of specialized writing techniques that could then be studied and emulated. If one considers the past six decades, then during the first three of those decades Chinese literature was virtually a complete blank within world literature—an utter wasteland. Its status was equivalent to a sheet of paper with mere scribbles on it, but without any enduring meaning. During the latter three decades, however, Chinese literature has undergone a dramatic transformation and has absorbed many outside elements, as a result of which it has demanded that your American works not resemble traditional eighteenth- and nineteenth-century literature. If a novel is able to tell a good story, create a satisfying narrative form, and reveal a broader society and lived environment, it will be considered a success. But Chinese readers during this period also want to find in the work traces of the author's independent personality; consequently, they might be reluctant to classify Salinger as a first-tier author, although they would certainly not hesitate to confer this status on any of the other authors discussed above.

This is because when it comes to other American authors from this period, it is not merely the content of their novels and their fictional characters that are perceived as being wild, but also their language, their narrative structure, and even their way of thinking. In the intertwined question of what and how to write, these authors appear to bring the two together under the concept of wildness — and although their respective forms of wildness may differ dramatically from one another, they nevertheless all maintain a wild, crazed, unbridled, rash, chaotic, and barbaric attitude with respect to traditional forms.

Even more importantly, for Chinese readers to embrace these "wild-child" works, they also had to embrace the authors' biographies. Accordingly, most of the authors were viewed as though they were characters within their own novels. This was especially true of authors belonging to the Beat Generation or the Lost Generation, and in China their works and life stories were interwoven with each other. For instance, it was said that, like the protagonist of *The Great Gatsby*, Fitzgerald was born poor but yearned for wealth and status, leading him to pursue the elite lifestyle until eventually it killed him. Later, Hemingway was famous for his wildness and obstinacy; consequently, his works reflect the principle that failure is just a different form of success. Kerouac was on the road when he composed *On the Road*, and to a certain extent his own unbridled personal life was even more a source of fascination for his readers than was his protagonist, Dean Moriarty. Similarly, it is not so much that Ginsberg and his book made it possible for his readers to hear the unrestrained scream of *Howl* but rather that *Howl* made it possible for readers to hear the screaming unrestraint of Ginsberg and his generation. The description in *Lolita* of the love between an adult professor (or what Chinese would call an intellectual) and a thirteen-year-old girl fed Chinese readers' hidden desires. When Miller described *Tropic of Cancer* as "a prolonged insult, a gob of spit in the face of Art, a kick in the pants to God, Man, Destiny, Time, Love, Beauty," he was giving voice to contemporary Chinese views of hypocrisy, morality, ethics, power, and order, as well as feudal, traditional, and contemporary politics and cultural and spiritual oppression — cursing them and kicking them in the butt. As for the more recent novel *Breakfast at Tiffany's*, Capote's yearning for and belief in material value accurately captures the adulation of wealth and material possessions among contemporary China's new generation of readers. The work's protagonist, Holly Golightly, can baldly display her love for money and jewels, thereby making Chinese readers feel that she is free and adorable in her wildness. Capote's own respect for natural instincts, however, is not reflected anywhere in the speech and actions of his protagonist.

By this point, American literature's new "wild-child" status had already begun to take shape. For Chinese readers, this form was not determined by any single work or group of works, nor by any single author or group of authors. Instead, it was the product of the collective influence of several generations of authors and countless individual works. This is comparable to the compassion and love found in great eighteenth- and nineteenth-century Russian literature, the social critique found in French and European modernist literature, and the mixture of fantasy and realism in the Latin American literary imagination. American literature during this period was characterized by a wild productivity that was made possible by the combined contributions of a nation, a people, and a great literary period, which collectively created a "beloved and respected wild child."

From the perspective of the nation's literary significance, this "wild child" may be seen as a form of independence and creativity; from a sociological perspective, it may be seen as an expression of America's free spirit and its individual freedom. The reason for the collective formation of this "wild-child" literature, and why it was so enthusiastically received in China, is that China's history and contemporary reality lack this sort of wildness at the level of China's literary production and lack this sort of freedom at the level of its people. The free life, existence, struggle, and even depravity of this "wild child" capture quite concisely the yearnings for freedom on the part of past, present, and future Chinese readers. One need not worry that American literature will be embraced and discarded in China as quickly as the French *nouvelle roman*, like Parisian fashion going in and out of season, and instead one should worry that when Chinese readers come to associate American literature with this "wild child of freedom," they may end up ignoring other good novels that happen to deviate from this model.

A BROAD YET SHALLOW INFLUENCE

No nation or region has produced as many authors with such a broad influence on Chinese readers as America. It must also be admitted, however, that among those American authors, there is not yet one who could be compared to Tolstoy and Balzac when it comes to their long and deep influence on the ways in which Chinese view the relationship between the individual and society. There is no American author comparable to Dostoevsky when it comes to his ability to lead Chinese authors into people's souls. There has been no American work comparable to Kafka's "The Metamorphosis" and *The Castle* when it comes to the way they have permitted readers to experience the fundamental solitude, loneliness, and hopelessness that characterize people's relationship to society. There has been no work comparable to García Márquez's *One Hundred Years of Solitude* when it comes to its ability to profoundly influence readers' understanding of literature while also transforming authors' attitudes and approach to literary production. Even Faulkner, despite being the most admired American author in China, has not yet had the same kind of profound and fundamental influence as these other authors. Why has American literature had such a broad yet comparatively shallow influence on the Chinese literary scene? Does the problem lie with American literature itself, or with Chinese readers, authors, and contemporary Chinese reality and history? These questions are difficult to answer, and I will not be able to offer a definitive response here. Given that our time is already up, I must conclude here with this question and hope that it offers everyone fruit for reflection and discussion.

5   My Thoughts on Literary Censorship and Controversy

In China we have a saying that reading a banned book on a snowy night is one of the true joys of life. From this, one can well imagine the kind of satisfaction that reading a banned book may bring—like candy locked up in a cabinet, it releases a sweet fragrance into solitary spaces. Whenever I travel abroad, I am invariably introduced as China's most controversial and most censored author. I neither agree nor disagree with this characterization—I'm not bothered by it, but neither do I feel particularly honored by it. Authors should be very clear that being banned is not synonymous with artistic success. Sometimes, being banned is equated with courageousness, and we can certainly understand Goethe's observation that without courage, there would be no art. If we were to extend this logic, we could even say that without courage, there would be no artistic creation. However, many readers view censorship and controversy *only* at the level of courage—particularly in relation to authors from China, the former Soviet Union, and other so-called third-world countries.

A BANNED BOOK IS NOT NECESSARILY A GOOD BOOK

Countless authors have had their books banned, including Aleksandr Solzhenitsyn, Boris Pasternak, Vladimir Nabokov, D. H. Lawrence, Jorge Luis Borges, Mario Vargas Llosa, Henry Miller, Milan Kundera, Salman Rushdie, Orhan Pamuk, and Ismail Kadare. If we were to stand in a library or open a computer to any page, these names may resemble a triumphant victory procession stretching from antiquity up to the present. However, the reason that everyone remembers these well-known names from the much longer list of banned authors is not only because their works were censored, but more importantly it is because these censored works were *great works*. As for those other authors who made enormous sacrifices in the name of freedom of speech, we must express our sincere respect for their sacrifices on behalf of their respective nations and to promote people's openness, advancement, freedom, democracy, and equality. However, if we consider these latter authors' works from a strictly aesthetic perspective, we must admit that we—or at least I—barely remember them at all. The reason for my inability to remember these authors, apart from my own blasted memory, is rooted in the inferior quality of the works themselves.

Art can be very cruel. Just as a day cannot be extended to thirty-six or forty-eight hours simply on account of someone's social status, similarly the achievement of an artwork does not increase simply on account of the oppression the artist happens to have faced. Even if the status of an artwork could be enhanced on these grounds, one day people might decide that this enhancement was inappropriate and secretly remove the work's extra stature. In contemporary China there are several—or even several dozen—books written every year that cannot be published because they have been censored or banned. Even if we resent this sort of censorship and are willing to go to great lengths to abolish it, we cannot automatically conclude that all books that have been censored are necessarily great works of art.

I know that when contemporary Chinese authors go abroad, and particularly when they travel to the United States, they like to talk about how their books have been criticized, censored, and banned—because they hope this will encourage foreign publishers to take interest in them. But I hope that my esteemed friends will forgive me when I say that censorship and controversy are not only a stain within the Chinese censorship system; they are also the most immediate means by which the West can approach Chinese works. However, this does not necessarily offer a standard for evaluating the artistic quality of the works in question. Several years ago, a Chinese author spent hundreds of thousands of yuan bribing the Chinese publishing industry so that it would criticize and ban his works. This hilarious example illustrates how censorship is truly a pathway to recognition, as opposed to being a standard of artistic quality. For this reason, whenever I am abroad and am introduced as China's most censored author, I simply remain silent, feeling neither pride nor pleasure in this description. I can only treat this sort of introduction as an inappropriate courtesy—such as when you encounter an acquaintance and offer your cheek to be kissed, and the acquaintance merely extends a hand.

As it happens, the first work of mine that Western readers were able to access was my banned novel *Serve the People!* Regardless of how you might assess this work, however, I don't believe it is particularly significant within the context of my overall oeuvre. It is merely a mark, event, and memory within my life and work, and it is definitely not a masterpiece. Readers who like *Serve the People!* should read *Hard Like Water.* I'm very pleased when people report that they like *Hard Like Water*, but when they praise *Serve the People!*, I can only smile. My 1994 collection *Summer Sunset* was also banned in China, but while this work is significant within the context of the genre of China's military literature and its contemporary tradition of realist fiction, it is less significant if considered within the context of my overall oeuvre. The broader the context, the harder it is to specify a work's significance. Of all my banned books, I hope that people would read *Dream of Ding Village* and *Lenin's Kisses*, not those earlier works. Similarly, when people discuss me, I prefer that they refer to me simply as an author, not as China's most controversial or most censored author.

My entire life, I have simply sought to produce good works and to be a good writer, and certainly have not aspired to become China's most controversial and most censored author.

IN CONTEMPORARY CHINA, IT IS ALWAYS SUSPICIOUS IF ONE WRITES FOR ONE'S ENTIRE LIFE AND NEVER BECOMES THE OBJECT OF CONTROVERSY

Irrespective of how Chinese authors might be discussed abroad, some people will claim that China's media and publishing industries are loose and free, and are endowed with "Chinese characteristics." At the same time, however, there are also people who exaggerate the dark side of China's censorship system to receive more attention. Although these authors may be as innocuous as a spring breeze when they are in China, whenever they go abroad, they invariably stress how controversial they are and how they have been censored, revised, and banned in China.

Actually, China's censorship system enjoyed a watershed moment around 1978. Before that year, when it came to freedom of expression and freedom of the press, the atmosphere resembled that of the White Terror period, with strict political restrictions, and anyone who exceeded these strictures automatically became subject to a "prison house of language" (this is sometimes the case even today). It was common for people to be imprisoned or executed. A case in point is Zhang Zhixin, who taught at the Chinese university where I am currently based. Given that, in 1968, he insisted on speaking the truth, revolutionaries therefore cut out his tongue. There were many similarly cruel and outrageous incidents during the Cultural Revolution. After China implemented the Reform and Opening Up Campaign in 1978, the nation's economy became significantly more open, but its political system remained half-closed. This is particularly evident when it comes to issues of freedom of speech. Compared with the freedom of speech found in the West, China has opened only one of its two previously closed windows—and although that window is sometimes wide open, at other times it is so tightly sealed that not even flies and mosquitoes can get through. Nevertheless, compared with the revolutionary dictatorship and the closed-off quality of the preceding thirty years, this sometimes-open and sometimes-closed window provided China's writers and intellectuals with a breath of fresh air. However, our problem is that even when some fresh air manages to enter through an opening in the window, writers may proceed to dance and sing within the space bounded by these four walls and no longer seek the blue skies, white clouds, flowing rivers, and vast fields that lie outside. This is why I believe that if any author writing under China's current political regime, cultural environment, and real fetters manages to produce a lifetime oeuvre that, from the perspective of its content or form, is never debated or denounced, much less censored, then *this* should definitely invite suspicion.

I once visited the home of an author who has received considerable attention in China and has won virtually all the government's major literary awards—including both the Mao Dun and Lu Xun prizes, as well as prizes for his essays, fiction, stage plays, and even film scripts. This author has written numerous works, and if you were to pile up all those wooden, glass, and metal awards and certificates, they would form an edifice even taller than the works themselves, to the point that they wouldn't even fit inside a single cabinet. Apart from the accolades received for his works, this author was as insulated from controversy and criticism as a plant growing in a greenhouse is insulated from the change of seasons. When we observe the pride that this author takes in the honors he has received, accordingly, we cannot help but feel a twinge of sorrow.

Being the object of controversy and censorship is never a good thing, nor is it, in itself, evidence of the inherent worth of the literary works in question. In the confused and cruel reality of contemporary China, however, to be censored may be taken as a mark of respect because it may be viewed as evidence of the author's courage and integrity. Meanwhile, an author who has *never* been the object of censorship and criticism, and who instead conforms to the political whims of this half-open and half-closed window, is not only inherently suspicious but furthermore is pathetic and even tragic.

China's literary scene can be compared to a sheep pen, and although the pen's gate may be slightly ajar, it is nevertheless still securely chained. Under these circumstances, the sheep in the pen have four options. First, they can obediently remain inside, waiting for their owner to praise or feed them. Second, they can ram the gate, although if they do, one can well imagine their fate. Third, because the gate is slightly ajar, a cunning and selfish sheep could use a technique of self-shrinkage to sneak out and taste some freedom, breathe some fresh air, and enjoy the scenery, but then return to the pen and sit tight like a fish entering water. Fourth, a magnanimous and upright sheep might wish to leave the pen but not be willing to shrink itself to do so, and instead it might use its bravery and wisdom, its horns and strength, to figure out a way to make its owner open the gate, or else it would use its own strength to force the gate open.

Although these are all sheep, they differ in that the first uses its weakness and cowardice to get fed, the second uses its irascibility to be cursed and beaten, the third uses its selfishness and hypocrisy to achieve a harmonious existence inside and outside the pen, and the fourth uses intelligence, bravery, and action to ensure (on behalf of itself and the others) that the gate will be opened and will never again be closed. In a pen where there is either no gate at all or where the gate is tightly closed, we respect the sheep that is willing to ram the gate. However, in a pen where the gate is slightly ajar, I would side with the sheep that uses bravery, intelligence, and action to try to get the gate to open freely.

We have proposed that in our current environment, in which the gap between writing and censorship is only half open, a Chinese author who never encounters any controversy whatsoever is definitely suspicious, although an author whose work is *always* met with controversy and censorship would also be suspect. As for myself, I would prefer to be an irascible and impetuous sheep rather than a meek and cowardly one that is regularly fed by its master. By the same token, I'd prefer to struggle to get the pen's gate to open freely so that everyone can pass through rather than attempt to contort myself so that I alone can squeeze in and out. I'd rather die trying to get the gate fully open than live by contorting myself to sneak in and out. If I'm unable to escape, at least I'd like to glimpse the outside world, and if I'm unable to glimpse the outside world, at least I'd like to be able to hear the wind, rain, footsteps, and laughter of the people outside. If we're unable to escape, or see or hear any of this, we should at least offer our silent respect to those sheep who are willing to ram the gate and sacrifice themselves so that it might be opened.

TO ATTEND TO THOSE THINGS TO WHICH THEY ARE NOT PERMITTED TO ATTEND, AUTHORS MUST HAVE HIGHER ARTISTIC ATTAINMENTS AND CREATIVITY

When it comes to topics of censorship, controversy, and criticism, we invariably focus too much on so-called sensitive issues. This is a trap into which even brave and righteous authors and intellectuals may fall. When an author's work lacks artistic value, he is like a painter who lacks both pigments and skill and who instead simply dips his brush in clear water. Or else he resembles a painter who has *too many* pigments, to the point that he doesn't know which ones to select or how to use them, and instead simply dumps them all directly onto the canvas—where each of the pigments may be dazzling in its own right, but art and technique disappear in this explosion of color.

It would be a mistake to separate pigments from painting technique.

It would similarly be a mistake to separate content from artistic method.

When a peasant is striving to obtain the largest possible harvest, he will select the best seeds and soil, and will plow the land with the most meticulous methods. There is no skilled peasant who does not sweat when plowing his fields, just as there is no field with a reasonably large harvest that has not been methodically plowed. It is often said that a skilled farmer is the land's best artist. As for literary works featuring so-called sensitive and realistic content, they need an even more precise, well-researched, and unique art and technique, the same way that when sowing particularly rich soil, one needs a skilled technique, because otherwise it would be like sending a boar with no sowing skills to scatter seeds, as a result of which the crop seeds and grass seeds would get mixed together, such that after a luxurious green field sprouts out of the rich soil the crops will quickly be devoured by weeds. The result might appear beautiful, but in fact it is nothing but weeds and wildflowers.

When writing about contemporary reality and history, when it comes to that "sensitive zone" that ideology and aesthetic policies have clearly designated as untouchable, most authors use an approach emphasizing circumvention, or the equivalent of a "line ball" in tennis, whereby they pursue their work within a sphere that is permitted and tolerated. For a long time, it has been the case that the most contemporary and real historical material has been left to those authors who are called fools (of course, there are also others who are too smart and calculating, and who want to use "sensitive" topics to achieve fame). These authors use their honesty and conscience to violate policy, politics, and ideology, to write about those histories, events, and individuals that the government has tried to erase from memory. However, one issue that has been ignored is that when authors use literature to pursue contemporary and historical topics they are not permitted to pursue, they are frequently driven by honesty and bravery, yet the truth of events is often transformed into a dictator capable of overturning everything—a surging and irrepressible passion that covers up this artistic imperative and ignores the fact that truth does not amount to common sense.

It is certainly not the case that China completely lacks honest and courageous authors. Indeed, there are many writers who have honestly and courageously examined many post-1949 historical and contemporary topics that have been officially designated as off-limits—such as who, during World War II, was resisting Japan and who was instead fighting in pursuit of power. These authors have also pursued a series of post-Liberation revolutionary movements, including the White Terror that the Anti-Rightist Campaign unleashed on intellectuals, the Great Iron-Smelting Campaign, the so-called Three Years of Natural Disaster following the Great Leap Forward, the decade-long catastrophe of the Cultural Revolution, as well as the student movement of 1989 and its now-forgotten conclusion.

Nevertheless, we currently have neither a great nonfiction masterpiece like *The Gulag Archipelago* nor a great novel like *Doctor Zhivago*. More than twenty million Chinese lost their lives during World War II, but unlike the West we don't have countless literary works reflecting on life and war, nor do we have works brimming with sympathy for the losses that the common people experience during war. Instead, virtually all our literature and art simply praise war, heroism, and the Party. Some films have recently begun to approach the topic of the Nanjing Massacre, but it turns out that these films are more concerned with fame, profit, and international prizes than with reflecting on war and expressing compassion for people's fate. On the topic of the Anti-Rightist Campaign and the Three Years of Natural Disaster, one author wrote the reportage novels *Goodbye, Jiabiangou* and *Dingxi Orphanage*, and that author's conscience and courage are such that all other Chinese authors, including myself, should bow down before her. However, regardless of whether these latter two works are treated as historical records or as fiction, their artistic weaknesses make readers feel sorrowful and heartbroken. Why is this? The simplest reason is that China's most talented and creative authors also have a vested interest in this society and are smart enough to avoid the historical and contemporary truths that they are not permitted to touch.

Most of these contemporary authors could be considered insiders, whereas those who possess conscience and courage find that, on account of the limitations of their attainments, creativity, and understanding of literature, they are unable to use their art—or use art itself—to grasp these enormous truths and histories. This is also why today, when we want to consider banned or forbidden works, not only must we interrogate and pursue our vantage point; we also need to question our own ability to master and depict these topics. When authors facing these sorts of forbidden topics produce controversial works, they need greater creativity than would be required for works about permitted topics. They must use this creativity not to avoid the censors or to sidestep the critique that they are pursuing sensitive topics simply because they are sensitive, and instead they should follow the logic that sensitive topics require creative approaches. This illustrates the simple fact that although many authors stick with artistically safe modes of composition within the realm of the permitted, when a minority of honest authors pursue forbidden realities and historical areas, they are not only doing so for the sake of their conscience but also for the sake of their art.

THAT WHICH IS BANNED WILL NOT NECESSARILY BE FORGOTTEN, AND THAT WHICH IS PERMITTED WILL NOT NECESSARILY PERSIST

If one agrees with the precept that one of the objectives of writing is to extend individual and collective memory, then it logically follows that as authors are drifting down the river of time, they will be able to enter or leave the river only in midstream. The river is much longer than the lives of those traveling down it, meaning that an author can traverse only a small portion of the river during his or her own lifetime. Therefore, when we assess an author's works, we find they are unable to extend humans' and humanity's memory of emotions and events. Meanwhile, as for the significance of the memories that these works seek to extend, it is not the author who has the final say but rather the river, time, and the future.

On this river that carries countless memories, one finds the following postulate:

That which is banned will not necessarily be forgotten, and that which is permitted will not necessarily persist.

In principle, one bans something in order that it be forgotten and affirms something so that it may persist. This is the objective for which all countries carry out nonartistic administrative interventions. China's classic novel *Dream of the Red Chamber* was initially viewed as a lascivious text that had to be banned, even though the memory of that era's emotions and spirit, and of the attractiveness of Chinese written characters, will continue to float down the river of time. Similarly, even today the great novel *The Plum in the Golden Vase* cannot be published or even printed in China, although the home of virtually every Chinese literatus has a copy that was printed in Taiwan, Hong Kong, or Macau. Even an artistically crude work like Li Yu's *The Carnal Prayer Mat* was later read and studied precisely because it had been previously banned. Conversely, contemporary China has far too many Red Classics, which are reprinted year after year because the Ministry of Education has designated them to be canonical works. Apart from the literary-historical significance of these Red Classics, however, I'm afraid they are moving further and further from society's "natural reading." We can easily imagine that the glow some Red Classics previously enjoyed in one era may become dimmed as society develops in a different direction, just as *Dream of the Red Chamber* eventually became canonized and widely disseminated once it was no longer banned.

Of course, just as banning something does not necessarily mean it will be forgotten and affirming it does not guarantee that it will persist, we could also say that banning something does not ensure that it will circulate and affirming it does not ensure that it will be preserved. Black and white, good and bad, canonical and commonplace, circulating and annulled—these various factors cannot be determined by simple binaries of being banned or published, of being negated or affirmed. However, when a work is assessed on a scale of being critiqued and being affirmed, the weight of conscience may at a certain point tilt the scale toward the side of being critiqued. This is not a speculation or shortcut, but rather it reflects readers' respect for honesty and their faith in writing, together with truth's gratitude for conscience. However, authors who are subject to critique cannot simply rely on their honesty and conscience, but instead they must also have a higher artistic pursuit and creativity. They must understand that by having faith in the pursuit of honesty, they will temporarily be subject to the principle of "being banned but not necessarily forgotten," yet only banned art possessing a unique creativity and a loving interrogation of the human spirit will be assured of becoming a more long-lasting memory and a landmark for which the human spirit, in its pain, is continually searching.

IN CHOOSING WHETHER TO BE ACCEPTED
OR SPURNED, I PREFER TO BE SPURNED

Virtually all countries throughout the world use a mundane scenario to illustrate the dilemma of choosing between two undesirable outcomes—namely, if your wife and mother were to fall into a river and you could save only one of them, whom would you save? This question sets up a moral trap: regardless of whom you try to save, you yourself will inevitably end up drowning in moralistic spittle.

If I were faced with this choice, I would save the person who would have the greatest significance for my family in the future. This is because my responsibility is not only to my mother and wife but also to my family. If in the future it is my mother who would be most beneficial to my family, then I would rescue my mother, but if it is my wife, then I would rescue my wife. As for the one who ends up being swept away by the churning river—if she could understand my predicament, this would be the greatest consolation for my spirit, but if she were to curse me while being swept away, I would be fated to carry this curse with me to my deathbed.

In any nation or society, even if we can't say that authors will automatically be praised and be able see their works affirmed, this is not a situation that authors would necessarily oppose or reject. In contemporary China, authors must choose between the equivalent of rescuing their mother or their wife. This is because, when faced with a combination of power and ideology, the market can be controlled by power. Power controls the markets, just as it drives the stock market. (Most) readers are also controlled by power, given that for decades it has been controlling all the nation's newspapers and television stations, as well as modern communication platforms like Weibo and WeChat.

(This morning, as I was reviewing my notes for this lecture, I read a newspaper article reporting that after a "rumor" has been reposted more than five hundred times on platforms like Weibo and WeChat, it thereby becomes subject to a new national law. In China, where more than two hundred million people use cell phones, for a piece of news to be reposted five hundred times is as easy as a drop of spittle fracturing into five hundred, five thousand, or even five hundred thousand droplets. Although rumors must necessarily be subject to legal review, the challenge is how to distinguish between actual rumors and mere exaggerations, between falsities and complete fabrications. In a world where things are often indeterminate, who will differentiate between rumors and mere exaggerations, between falsities and complete fabrications? If the truthful revelation and exposure are qualities of rumor, then is not exaggerated praise also a kind of rumor?)

When all media outlets are managed and controlled by the state, then (virtually) all readers will similarly be managed and unified, as well as folk entertainment and misery. Today, China lets you "party till you drop," but it does not permit you to reflect critically on issues; it lets you believe in money and elevate the worship of money to an almost divine level, but it does not allow you freedom of belief. With literature, there are also some things that are permitted and others that are not. For instance, you are permitted to pursue goals based on the principles that the reader comes first, the market is paramount, enjoyment is eternal, and the ideal is pure art, pure technique, and aestheticism. However, you are not permitted to choose the exploration of artistic truth or literature's unremitting inquiry into the reality of the human soul. People who praise these principles will be commended, whereas those who question them will be restrained. This produces two kinds of situations, in that it takes the richest and most complicated reality and under the control of a shapeless power divides it into one set of writings that can be accepted by virtually everyone and another set that is rejected by most people. In making this division, power sometimes intrudes directly, as in the case of virtually all literary awards and literary censorship, but more often it operates indirectly, via market cultivation, people's reading pleasure, and authors' pursuit.

When authors' writerly pursuit, combined with elements associated with the market, pleasure, and readers, together with pure literature, aestheticism, technicalism, and positive energy, come together to form a collectively accepted camp, the authors with the most talent and prospects and the greatest ability to produce a great work will be accepted, and a minority of authors will be rejected. When this minority of authors is cast into the masses and viewed as the opposite of literature, they will be categorized as nonliterary and left to the side. At this point the porous boundary between literature and nonliterature will disappear, and all that will remain will be a distinction between works that are widely accepted and those that are clearly rejected. Therefore, an author will find himself in the position of the person on the riverbank trying to decide whether to rescue his mother or his wife, and regardless of whether he selects the market and his readers or so-called pure art, aestheticism, and technicalism, he will inevitably be caught in a trap of morality and fame and will drown in moralistic spittle.

If someone is going to be forced to make this choice on the riverbank, let that choice be to be cast aside and drowned in moralistic spittle.

I must choose not only between my mother and wife but also between who will be most helpful in helping me rebuild my broken family and household.

In the process of choosing between being accepted and being cast aside, I choose to be cast aside and risk being drowned in moralistic spittle.

When power aligns readers, the market, and pure art into a unified front, these elements do not share much with one another, but instead they achieve a state of co-victory, co-prosperity, and coexistence, whereas other writing becomes minoritized, contested, and banned. After all these divisions and classifications, however, in the end you are not actively choosing, but rather you are being chosen. You are not actively advancing, but rather you are being pushed forward after having been chosen. It is not that you don't wish to interact with a mass readership, but rather that a mass readership is cultivated and readers are defined, whereas your readers, because they are classified as a minority, are drowned in other people's moralistic spittle. The configuration has already been formed, and given that one is going to be chosen anyway, why not choose for oneself? Therefore, let me face the majority—let me stand in a position of having been rejected by most readers—and welcome those who want to come while letting the others leave. In this way, I hope to become someone who uses a pen filled with the blood of reality and the moralistic spittle of the masses to create his own literary tomb.

MY LITERARY ROAD INEVITABLY BECOMES NARROWER AND NARROWER

Time, age, reality, and the environment have left me feeling empty, vain, and ponderous. I no longer assume that China's contemporary reality can be significantly improved, and I certainly don't assume that literature will be able to change that reality. Even if I can't change reality, at the very least I hope that reality will not change me. Regardless of how hard I try, I'll never be able to change reality, although at the same time I recognize that reality is constantly transforming me, my literature, and my literary perspective.

Virtually all my friends and colleagues praise my works from the period in the late 1990s when I wrote *Streams of Time, Marrow*, and *The Years, Months, Days*, and they ask why I didn't continue writing in that manner. To this I laugh and reply, "As the saying goes, after you pass that village, you won't see that shop again." Why is this so? It is because China's current era is no longer the one in which I wrote those works, nor is China's current reality the same as it was then. My reality and state of mind have changed, and one's writing must necessarily be grounded in one's current reality and state of mind. The issue is that reality has changed me and my literature, not that my literature has created, shaped, transformed, or maintained that reality.

After finishing *Streams of Time*, I wrote *Hard Like Water*. However, the censors deemed *Hard Like Water* to be "Robbe-Grillet respect to both red [revolution] and yellow [sex]." Had it not been for the fact that a representative from my publisher, who was serving as the book's editor, went to Beijing and pulled all sorts of strings, this novel would definitely have been banned. Everyone regards *Lenin's Kisses* as an extraordinary work, yet it resulted in my being kicked out of the army. When *Serve the People!* was translated into numerous different languages, foreign publishers would invariably include, for publicity purposes, a reference—on either the front or back cover—to the work's having been banned in China. Later, many readers asked why, after *Serve the People!* created such a controversy, did I then decide to write *Dream of Ding Village*. Was this not a case of going against the current and trying to seize an opportunity to gain fame? What these readers didn't realize was that it was precisely because of the problems surrounding *Serve the People!* that I decided to write *Dream of Ding Village*. This is because I wanted to take the initiative and present myself to my readers. I wanted to show everyone that I love life, reality, and everyone in that reality. I resolved to write in this way because I wanted to display my devotion to real life—I thought that in the writing of *Dream of Ding Village*, my tolerance for contemporary reality and history, together with the enormous compromises and concessions I had made on behalf of history, would convey my enthusiasm for reality and my love of people. In the end, however, following the publication of *Dream of Ding Village*, this same love ultimately became the work's tomb. Not only was the novel banned after publication, but furthermore I came to be viewed as someone who was deliberately going against the current.

I could write an entire book about the controversies surrounding my works, but after a lengthy reflection, I have arrived at the following specific conclusions:

First, when works by modern Chinese authors have aroused controversy or been censored, this is usually not a result of the authors' own actions. These controversies are not something that authors seek out, but rather they are something that society needs.

Second, controversy and censorship are not good things, but they are also not necessarily bad. If an author is controversial, this demonstrates that at least he possesses integrity and magnanimity. To the extent that some authors have integrity, we should preserve their works. On the other hand, given that authors don't have the ability to alter society or reality, their works are ultimately less influential than a single remark in an official document or a gesture by someone in power. Given that an author's writings cannot change reality, we must simply ask that reality not change the author. We must try to help ensure that the qualities of integrity and truth in the author's works might endure.

Third, as for an author's ability to endure, one hopes this will not result in the author's becoming increasingly distanced from society, the environment, and most readers. Sometimes persistence is not merely persistence, but it is also an opposition to a consolidated position. I have gradually come to understand that because you persist and don't want to change, you must continuously be the object of controversy. If you persist but find that the controversy around you has stopped, that will be because it was not you but rather society itself that has changed. But that is such a distant eventuality! It is as difficult to imagine as a scenario where an egg and a rock collide and the egg remains intact while the rock shatters.

To tell the truth, I don't imagine that the egg would ever shatter the rock, and instead I simply hope that the shattered egg may retain some of its original freshness and that its yolk and egg white may remain bright.

That way, when readers—or at least a minority of readers—pass by, they will not be so put off. People will continue to engage in controversy and censorship, but this is irrelevant to you. You simply want to write—to write good works based on your understanding of people, the world, and literature. You simply hope that the powerful and prosperous society will not change you and that when you become a shattered egg, the egg white and yolk will retain their freshness.

That is all. From now on, I ask readers to stop describing me as China's most controversial and censored author. Instead, I request that you simply say that I am a Chinese author. It is enough to say that I'm an author with some basic rectitude and independence.

6 My Literary Review Book

When someone is in love, we always want to see how much they are willing to do for their loved one. This is a commonsensical and satisfying approach. However, there is also another kind of love that invites a different mode of evaluation. When someone's love is excessive, they won't remember what they have done for their loved one, and instead they will continually criticize themselves for what they *failed* to do and what they could have done better.

Love that leaves one feeling satisfied can be regarded as normal, whereas that which leaves one feeling guilty is a kind of bitterness. With the latter, love produces bitterness, and bitterness produces love.

When it comes to my relationship to own writing, I feel that my love probably approaches this sort of bitterness. When sitting alone in my study and reviewing my published works, I often ask myself, *Isn't this all garbage? Will anyone still be interested in reading these books in another five or ten years, not to mention after I'm dead?* Because I'm constantly doubting and questioning myself, I have developed a kind of hatred and hopelessness that continually makes me lose confidence in my own writing. Because my conviction that I have not written well brings me pain and regret, I have no choice but to experiment with a new (or at least what I believe to be new) kind of writing.

A famous Chinese author bought a copy of *Lenin's Kisses* less than two months after it was published. Upon finishing just a few pages, however, he ripped it up and cursed, "I'll never read another of his works as long as I live!" I'm not sure what it was about my novel that infuriated this author, whom I respect, nor do I have any idea what I might have done to offend him. Although my writing may well contain some wild, blunt, and impetuous elements, I believe I am basically a kind and prudent person. If I've ever offended anyone with my writings, I certainly hope I've made up for it in how I treat people in real life. Nevertheless, I really have no idea how I might have disrespected that friend who ripped up my novel. Therefore, when I later reread *Lenin's Kisses* and my other works, I struggled to determine where I hadn't written well enough. I began to engage in a process of self-questioning and self-critique, continually asking myself, *Are you a plausible author? Have you written even one or two good works in your entire life? What kind of problems do your works have?* As I asked myself these questions like a judge interrogating a defendant, I came to recognize many mistakes, and my biggest regrets include the following.

ALTHOUGH FACED WITH A RICH AND COMPLEX CHINESE REALITY, I FIND THAT MY WRITING APPEARS SIMPLE AND BIASED

I have long contended that no country's reality is more complex and absurd than China's. The things that occur in real life in China are almost more extraordinary than the fictional scenarios dreamed up by authors in other countries. When I first made this observation, I was afraid people would think I was grandstanding, but now virtually all Chinese authors feel the same way as I do. It is now conventional wisdom that Chinese authors' literary imagination is no match for the richness and complexity of real life.

For instance, who could have imagined that a game of hide-and-seek in a holding cell could have resulted in a college student getting killed after his head was smashed into a wall? Or that less than a year after opening, a medical clinic would admit more than a thousand patients and have a death rate of over 10 percent, with more than ten people on average dying every month?

Who could have imagined that for years Shaanxi's "black brick kilns" would have been using deaf-mute workers to carry bricks out of kilns that reached temperatures of over 40 degrees Celsius?

Who could have imagined that more than ten thousand pig carcasses would be found in Shanghai's Huangpu River or that countless dead ducks would be found floating down a river in Hangzhou?

Who could have imagined that after a provincial high court justice known as an exemplary cadre and anticorruption official died suddenly in an accident, it would be revealed that he had more than a hundred million yuan in savings, four wives (each with a legal marriage certificate), and six children?

When something unusual happens once, it can be attributed to chance, but if ten or twenty unusual incidents occur in succession, it is reasonable to conclude that they may well be related. Moreover, when monstrous incidents occur on a monthly, weekly, and even daily basis in the same territory, we have no choice but to conclude that the territory—in this case, China—has a serious problem.

China's economy is developing at a breakneck speed, and thousands of miles of new roads are being constructed every day. The changes that humans and human emotions are undergoing almost defy belief. Today's authors must recognize not only contemporary China's vitality but also the unbelievable distortions that this vitality has produced. They must recognize that the nation's development and prosperity are masking a pervasive sorrow. Regardless of whether people live in urban or rural areas, they are all busy pursuing money, vanity, and a beautiful future, even as they hurtle toward death and their souls slip into darkness. They become living people with dead souls. Contemporary authors find that their literary imagination is simply not up to the task of describing these dead souls, this vigorous but distorted contemporary reality, this absurd and unbelievable darkness, and this legendary reality. Authors find that they are unable to master this rapid development and the resulting distortions of people's lives.

To put it simply, real life is like a thorny wilderness that we try to enter while wearing only sandals. These sandals won't allow us to reach the interior of this wilderness, nor will they permit us to observe its new developments and entanglements, contradictions and collapses, vitality and pain. Because we don't dare—and neither are we able—to enter this new wilderness, we must settle for standing at the edge and speculating about what is inside. As a result, we lack the sort of unforgettable experience that comes from reality itself, as well as the sort of feeling that is so unforgettable that it hurts your soul. Our writing, accordingly, cannot help but take the form of a simple and biased "bystander literature."

For a while, I felt quite bitter toward that friend who ripped up his copy of *Lenin's Kisses*. At the same time, however, I was also very grateful, because in ripping up my book he thereby allowed me to recognize China's reality and the position of my writing within that reality. Ever since, I have repeatedly reflected on reality's complexities and absurdities. It is only when I compare my works to contemporary reality, and particularly when I attempt to base my works on this reality, that I realize how simple and crude my writing actually is. It was also from this point that I began to pay more attention to this colleague's own works. He was indeed a good writer, and his works had many qualities that I was unable to achieve. Meanwhile, compared with the richness of contemporary reality, my own works such as *Hard Like Water*, *Lenin's Kisses*, *Dream of Ding Village*, *The Four Books*, and *Ballad, Hymn, Ode* are like a single tree next to an enormous forest or a single bowl of water next to a vast river. Even today, I feel embarrassed when readers say that Yan Lianke's works have more contemporary significance than those of other Chinese authors. This is because I know that contemporary reality is as muddy and turbulent as the Yellow River, whereas my novels are as limpid as water in a shallow well, so clear that you can see your reflection in it. It is certainly good for well water to be clear, but when you describe the Yellow River as though it were well water, that is not merely a failure; it is an embarrassment to life, literature, and reality.

Some people say that Yan Lianke's novels always contain an anxious, discomfiting quality when they approach contemporary reality. When I hear this, however, I'm not sure whether it is a compliment or a critique. When faced with an absurd reality, should an author stand before that reality and attempt to examine and interrogate it, or should he instead stand inside it and engage in a process of naturalistic description devoid of any rational judgment? Regardless of whether I use objective description or rational critique to approach contemporary reality, contemporary people, and people's souls, the result inevitably feels simple and crude. In contrast to authors like Dostoevsky and Kafka, who approached people's lives with love and compassion, or Camus, who approached reality with cold detachment, by the time you get to contemporary Chinese authors like myself, those experiences and attitudes acquire a certain untimely quality. This is because contemporary China is completely different from eighteenth-century Europe, nineteenth-century Russia, or even twentieth-century America, and whether one uses critique and satire or compassion and love to approach contemporary China and its people, the result will inevitably appear simple and biased.

A difficult question confronting Chinese authors involves what kind of attitude they should adopt in approaching the reality of contemporary China and its people. It is not simply the case, as is often claimed, that we've lost the ability to master complex reality. Instead, I believe that, from the perspective of our experience in reading, writing, and reflecting, Chinese authors of my generation—which is to say, those born in the fifties and sixties—have already reached the point where we are most able to master reality, characters, stories, and emotions. However, what we lack is an appropriate attitude with which to approach contemporary China's complex, contradictory, and absurd reality. We have lost the means to understand reality and we lack an appropriate standpoint from which to approach it.

If we were to use any earlier literary attitude to approach contemporary China, the result would inevitably be simple, crude, and rough.

The reason I feel anxious every time I sit down to write is because I don't know how to confront the reality of contemporary China. It is not that I don't have any stories to write, nor is it that I lack the ability to write those stories, but rather that I don't have an appropriate attitude and perspective with which to approach contemporary China's rich, absurd, and bizarre reality. Earlier attitudes and perspectives, even if filled with love and compassion, now appear too simplistic—like an inadequate compromise following a sense of hopelessness.

THE WEAKNESS WITHIN INDEPENDENCE

I find that as I've aged, I've become more tolerant.

The same way that, following the loss of a loved one, one comes to better understand the shortcomings of one's relatives, I often think that even if my mother and father were thieves, they would still be my parents, and even if my sister and brother-in-law were murderers, I would probably still try to defend them.

I know I shouldn't be critical of other Chinese authors, and I certainly don't have the standing to critique what they write or how they write it. This is because contemporary China is a rich soil that produces all sorts of different writers, and all kinds of writing approaches are acceptable. But as I get older and weaker, I become increasingly critical when it comes to my own writing. To be critical of one's own writing is to be independent and awakened. For instance, I know I am easily seduced by power, fame, and fortune—and this is because after someone who was born into poverty manages to achieve some success, it is very easy for them to succumb to the appeal of fame, fortune, and power.

China's short-lived emperor Li Zicheng led a hard life, and after he finally achieved success, he succumbed to the seductions of status and corruption. Similarly, the modern Chinese poet Guo Moruo was talented and elegant, but this led him to lack independence, worship power and status, and prematurely exhaust his talent. When it comes to American authors like F. Scott Fitzgerald, Jack Kerouac, and Truman Capote, I feel that although their writing does not lack independence, as individuals they nevertheless had many shortcomings, and their eventual downfall was a result of the temptation and weakness with which they approached life. As for myself, I certainly can't be discussed in the same breath with these other figures, although unfortunately I fear I share some of the limitations that characterized their writings and their lives.

In short, I feel that my writing lacks independence and my life is marked by weakness.

In 2011 I encountered the sort of "forced demolition" incident that one finds only under conditions of social development. The government had sold me my house but then, on the pretext that no one was living there, subsequently designated the building to be an illegal structure and ordered that it be demolished. I repeatedly petitioned China's highest officials to address this matter and tried to use the power of the public and the media to defend my rights and resist the demolition. In the end, however, I fell silent, and it was not merely police intimidation that led me to compromise, but more importantly it was my own weakness of character.

After the controversy surrounding *Serve the People!*, when writing *Dream of Ding Village* I undertook a rigorous process of self-censorship.

The version of the latter novel that everyone reads today is a passable work, but only I know how rigorously I censored myself while writing it. Only I know what kind of novel it might have been had I not been working under a regime of fear, vigilance, and self-censorship.

Meanwhile, *The Four Books* was never published in China, but it was the product of my decision that if I couldn't avoid external censorship, I would at the very least try to liberate myself from a process of self-censorship. In writing the latter work, I developed my independent character. When it comes to writing and publishing in China, one cannot say that authors who are able to publish every work they write are necessarily weak and lack independence. However, when it comes to my own writing, it is clear that if I want to publish my works, I'll have to compromise with the censorship system and will need to sacrifice piece after piece of my independent character.

We often hear Chinese authors—both at home and abroad—claim that there are ways of getting around the censorship system. For instance, given that in China you can't mention June Fourth, netizens instead often use expressions like *May thirty-fifth* or *the fourth day of June*. Not only is this true, but it's also humorous and wise. More importantly, however, it also represents a kind of weakness and compromise. It is the self-healed wound suffered by people's independence after power takes a bite out of it. This does not make me feel amused or proud of the Chinese people, nor does it convince me that they are wise. Instead, I simply feel bitter that their independence has been undermined and feel frustrated that their integrity has been undercut. When an author doesn't attempt to say June Fourth, 1989, and instead uses a roundabout expression like "May thirty-fifth of the year immediately preceding 1990," he has already lost his independence. You have already won a puny, safe, and self-satisfied position for your weakness—just as Lu Xun's Ah Q took the curses he had hidden in his heart and used them against society and his enemies.

This realization brings me a tremendous sense of pain and sorrow.

I am determined not to be someone who refers to June Fourth as "May thirty-fifth." This is not necessarily because I want to be different from others but rather because I think that although power can break my legs and cripple my independence, it would be best if I no longer try to use weakness to compensate for that crippled independence.

Chinese authors should be grateful for the role that Taiwan and Hong Kong have played in supplementing mainland publications. This is especially true of Taiwan, which has gone to considerable effort to preserve Chinese literature and culture, the way a wise and compassionate monk feels love for all beggars. Taiwan's and Hong Kong's presses have published virtually all the worthy works by contemporary mainland authors, even if they are not profitable—and this is particularly true of those works that have been censored or banned in China. The respect that Taiwan's publishing industry has for the original integrity of our culture resembles the unqualified love that a mother has for her children regardless of their appearance or ability. The supplementary role played by this publication system helps nourish Chinese authors' independence and permits them to experience a degree of self-liberation and freedom even under a regime of self-censorship. After all, many authors find a bridge enabling them to cross to the other shore, so in their writing they can have a freer attitude with which to reach a true artistic peak. After completing their works, they can give the complete manuscript to Taiwan or Hong Kong publishers and then offer a censored version to a mainland Chinese publisher. This represents a compromise of the authors' independence, but it also supplements their weakness. Therefore, China's authors and readers, together with future literature and culture, should bow in gratitude to Taiwan's and Hong Kong's publishing industries.

As for an author like myself, who lacks independence when it comes to my writing while also having an excess of weakness when it comes to my life, I am particularly grateful to Taiwan's publishers. Had it not been for their commitment to publishing the complete versions of my texts, I would not have been so quick to decide to release myself from a regime of self-censorship, nor would my artistic dreams and courage be what they are today.

Of course, I am grateful that when power makes it difficult for a Chinese author to publish in China, it still allows him to publish abroad. This represents a significant improvement over the situation thirty years ago, when if an author arranged to have his works published abroad after being banned in China, this would have been grounds for imprisonment and even execution. Now things are different, and this kind of practice is tolerated. This permits an author's hard work to be preserved while also allowing him to maintain his integrity and independence. After an author loses one leg, power permits him to continue standing on the other, and it doesn't force him to collapse onto a kneeling mat and genuflect abjectly.

For this, I am very, very, very grateful!

IS THERE A FULLY INDEPENDENT NARRATIVE PATH?

When faced with the vastness of literature and classics, what worries authors the most is not the complexity of reality and the oppressiveness of power, nor is it whether they will be permitted to write. Instead, what worries them is *how* they should write. Once when I was with the Japanese poet Shuntarō Tanikawa, I suggested that he was virtually the only person in the world who could manage to live comfortably in Japan while relying solely on royalties from his poetry. Although his writing was not as lucrative as Haruki Murakami's, it was nevertheless significantly more lucrative than that of even the Nobel laureate Kenzaburō Ōe. From this, one can tell how well-known Tanikawa was in Japan and around the world. When he and I discussed China's writing environment, its publishing system, and its authors' independence, he was initially silent for a long time, then he said earnestly, "Chinese authors are simply too fortunate. If a work expresses the author's independence, it has the potential to make power nervous and anxious. This is really something to be envied."

I was silent.

I didn't know how to respond to this great poet.

But I did know that the reason Tanikawa had earned such broad adulation in China was not because his poems exhibit the sort of independence that one finds in the works of Aleksandr Solzhenitsyn, George Orwell, Jack Kerouac, Allen Ginsberg, Joseph Heller, Henry Miller, and Vladimir Nabokov, but it is because these poems have a distinct rhythm and narrative style, combined with an awareness of humanity and the world. Sometimes there is a difference between an author's independence and his unique artistic narrative, but every novelist aspires to a perfect synthesis between the two. In this respect, *The Gulag Archipelago* and *1984* are counterexamples of works that were great despite failing to achieve this balance, while *Lolita* is an example of a work that achieved this balance while still not being great.

Let me return to Chinese literature and my own writings. Even though I realize that my works lack independence, I frequently wonder whether, if the day were to come when Chinese authors could finally achieve the independence they seek, would they thereby attain a unique narrative style?

I ask myself:

Are your stories really your own?

Are your characters, plots, and subplots characteristic of China, or are they completely original?

Did you create your linguistic signs yourself, or did you harvest them from other people's language? When you use the phonemes for the numbers 1, 2, 3, 4, 5, 6, and 7, do your lyrics sound fresh, strange, and beautiful, or do they sound pleasing but all too familiar?

Have you ever attempted to create a completely new narrative structure? Did that attempt succeed or fail?

Most Chinese critics use Western literary theories to corroborate the artistry of Chinese novels, or they mechanically apply Western theories to Chinese novels. This is like a referee who always says that our opponents kicked the ball directly into their own goal or accidentally kicked the ball off a member of our team and into our goal—but that either way we should still be awarded the point and celebrate this as an "own goal." I don't know whether it is the case that China's critics don't have any literary theories they can call their own, or whether it is because China's novelists have never written genuine "Chinese novels" and therefore critics have no choice but to use Western theories to analyze them. An "own goal" is never a good thing, even when it is our opponent's "own goal" that gives us the victory.

We might lift the trophy, but we'll still have a bitter taste in our hearts.

Chinese novelists shouldn't critique the critics, and instead they should reassess their own so-called creations.

We must acknowledge that our contemporary writings have absorbed too much from Western knowledge and Western technique.

We must understand that the question is not what we should absorb from Western literature but rather what we should discard.

Given that we should find our own way, why not backtrack and follow our own literary path? This does not require that we return to Chinese tradition, but it suggests that after we have absorbed enough Western knowledge and techniques, we can more clearly recognize the greatness of Eastern culture as well as Eastern tradition's future significance. Then, with one foot in the West and the other in the East, we can create a distinctive literary understanding and literary methodology that truly belong to the East, to China, and to the authors themselves.

We must realize a literary modernity that belongs to China and to ourselves.

World literature must include a narrative order that belongs to the East and to ourselves.

When readers and critics initially described my own novels as absurd, satirical, black humor, magical realism, or postmodern, I was secretly pleased because this suggested a connection between Chinese and Latin American literature. But when readers and critics say those things about my works now, I instead feel frustrated. The more earnestly they say these things, the more frustrated I become—the way that a child who has committed plagiarism feels more flustered the more he is praised for his work. I once proposed the concept of mythorealism to describe a certain tendency in Chinese literature and my own writing, and I even developed this concept in a small volume of so-called literary theory titled *Discovering Fiction*. In addition to discussing my individual perspective on nineteenth- and twentieth-century world literature, I proposed that Chinese fiction is characterized by an Eastern quality of mythorealism. This proposal was mocked by many Chinese critics, but their disdain was like a deity who looks down on a poor temple worshipper for having only a single incense stick. However, I—this poor temple worshipper enveloped in incense smoke—pray that we may achieve some resistance to and release from Western literature, while also recognizing that complete release would be impossible.

What this poor temple worshipper wants to argue is that even as Western narrative hovers over one's head like a black cloud, an author still must struggle to part this cloud and seek a ray of sunlight. Or, to put this another way, even if Western narrative is shining down on your head like a bright sun, you must find a Chinese lotus or cattail leaf and hold it over your head like a parasol.

I feel ashamed that I have not done a better job of retreating and reconstructing, but I nevertheless frequently engage in self-critique and struggle to advance.

To improve and advance, an author must frequently engage in a process of self-critique.

Every time I finish a book, I always sit for a while and reflect on the work's shortcomings; then I get together with friends to discuss its possibilities. My reading of works by other Chinese authors is limited and unsystematic, but when it comes to my own writing, my primary demand is that I recognize where I wrote poorly or not well enough. I know that apart from the areas where I lack the ability to master—or even clearly understand—the richness and complexity of contemporary Chinese reality, my literature is not independent enough and I am not strong enough. I have not yet established a truly distinctive narrative system, and amid all the inconsistencies between literature and real life, including the politics contained by real life, the gap between "mythos" and daily life, and the insufficient integration of technique and content, there is also the repetition of language, plot, and thought, and so forth—all this needs reflection and reform, effort and new creation. However, although I have already reached an age at which it is easy to engage in self-critique, it is not so easy for me to reform myself or create something new.

Time does not forgive, but the human heart can strengthen itself.

In this fairly general literary self-critique, I will continue to think and reflect. I don't ask that everything be corrected, but I do ask that there be thoughtful revision and correction:

The revolution has not yet succeeded. Our comrades must continue to struggle!

7 The Distinctiveness of Writing in China

When I talk to non-Chinese readers like yourselves, I often find that you are interested in hearing about the distinctive characteristics not only of me as an author but also of my country—and particularly details that go beyond what you see on the television, read about in the newspapers, and hear about from tourists.

I know that China's international reputation is like that of a young upstart from the countryside who has money but lacks culture, education, and knowledge. Of course, in addition to money, this young upstart also possesses things like despotism and injustice, while lacking democracy and freedom. The result is like a wild man loaded with gold bullion but who also has shabby clothing, rude behavior, and bad breath, and who never plays by the rules. If an author must write under the oversight of this sort of individual, how should that author evaluate, discuss, and describe him?

To address this question, we will first consider the distinctive writing conditions faced by contemporary Chinese authors.

LIGHT AND SHADOWS BENEATH A HALF-OPEN AND HALF-CLOSED WINDOW

The entire world knows that China's economy has recently undergone a process of reform and opening up, whereas the relationship between China's advanced economic system and its conservative political system is like the fable in which the tortoise beats the hare who stops to take a nap. In the race between China's economic and political reform, the economy is currently surging ahead while politics stops to take a nap.

In contrast to China's economic tortoise, its political hare has not merely slowed down or stopped; it has even turned around and headed back whence it came. For instance, in discussing China's freedom of expression and ideological emancipation, people sometimes refer to the nation's prison house of language—and even if it is not technically a prison, it is at the very least a cage. Although the nation's economic window is either open or in the process of being opened and its political window is either closed or in the process of being closed, its culture looks around in confusion at the resulting play of light and shadows. The nation's literature— which is to say, authors' writings—is also stuck in this intermediary zone. Meanwhile, the billion-plus Chinese people who gather beneath these windows to breathe and survive find that the brightness and warmth here are unpredictable; consequently, their souls, spirits, and hearts become increasingly variable, decadent, and dark.

For the past several decades, China has demonstrated that the success of a planned economy lies not so much in the planning of the economy itself but rather in the planning of people's hearts. The ultimate objective of economic planning is not economic prosperity itself but rather control over the national and political aspects of people's souls. In a market economy, the market includes not only the economy proper but also people's souls and the freedom that must be banished for the sake of economic development. Because of the needs of power and politics, people's freedom cannot strictly follow the rise and fall of the economy. When the economic window is open, the political window will be closed, and ideological power will be concentrated. People's spirits will resemble a patch of grass struggling to grow in the intermittently light and dark area beneath these partially open and partially closed windows. Because there is insufficient light and irregular wind here (although it is certainly not the case that there is no light or wind at all), when this patch of grass manages to glimpse some light and wind, it will fight to secure them, and otherwise it will gasp and struggle in their absence.

This is the situation in contemporary China. The economic window is open and the political window is closed, and culture wanders in the intermediate zone between the two. Contemporary literature approaches the flourishing economy as though hugging a fireball and approaches the ubiquitous politics of contemporary reality as though embracing an enormous chunk of ice.

Politics expects that you write about the existence of that hot, bright, and visible so-called positive energy while also attending to the existence of that which, on the surface, appears to be a form of negative energy—including a reality that either cannot be seen or else doesn't even exist. In this intermediate zone, all Chinese, including children from preschool forward (but excluding infants, who are of course innocent and pure), are influenced by what they see and hear. For instance, children all know that teachers will respond favorably if they are offered gifts. Meanwhile, if an old man collapses in the street, it is only natural that bystanders will help him, but when the old man responds by accusing the bystanders of having knocked him down and demands compensation from them, this becomes a special kind of incident—a legal case. Given that the frequency of these sorts of incidents has recently increased, we cannot help but suspect that these apparent victims must hold darkness in their hearts. Accordingly, now if someone collapses or is hit by a car, passersby will often hurry away as though they didn't see anything, and although we may find this situation unreasonable, at least we can understand it. This illustrates how, in contemporary China, people's souls have become numb and dark.

What is bred under the open window of the economy is capital, desire, and evil, and what is bred under the closed window of politics is corruption, greed, and contempt for others. People's hearts become deformed, distorted, and absurd. If an author wants to realistically describe people's deepest souls, this is his God-given responsibility, and if the author gives this up, he will no longer have any need to exist. Meanwhile, the people who control when, how, and to what extent the two windows should be open or shut also control authors' pens and remind them what they can and can't write. These people constantly remind authors that the light of one person's heart has positive energy and should be discussed in detail, but the darkness of another person's heart cannot be discussed because that might touch on the underlying reason why that person's heart is dark in the first place.

Meanwhile, for the sake of their survival, honor, and status, the authors living under these partially open and partially closed windows (and under the supervision of the people overseeing the windows) must adopt one of the following three writing methods.

First, there is writing that welcomes light. When you see and obtain light, you write to welcome it. The more you write about light, the brighter your writing will become, and the more prestige and status will illuminate your life—the same way that sunlight shines into your room when you open a window in the morning.

Second, there is writing that borrows light. People who write to borrow light are all talented Chinese authors with a certain degree of conscience and wisdom. Because these authors are unwilling to write to welcome light but are also unwilling to give up their internal artistic sentiment, they have no choice but to borrow light from others. As a result, they always have a feeling of guilty gratitude and don't attempt to explore the reality behind that half-closed window. They know that behind that window there lies the greatest truth, but because they have borrowed light, they resemble someone who—after using someone else's tools or eating someone else's food—naturally won't excavate the foundations of that other person's house. Therefore, these authors reach a tacit agreement that they will remain in the boundary zone between light and darkness and will use an artistic balance to complete a "literary idea" that belongs to both regions.

Third, there is writing that transcends light to reach the truth of darkness. This kind of writing is risky because you not only betray light after transcending it but also betray all the authors and works positioned in the intermediary zone between light and darkness. Furthermore, everything located in the light and at its margins is visible, whereas the truth of that darkness remains invisible and can only be felt. Therefore, your writing is not something everyone can recognize, and instead it leads people to doubt, argue, and spurn. This is also why writing that transcends light to reach darkness, and which proceeds from the illuminated window to the area beneath the dark window—this kind of writing requires not only courage but also talent and creativity. You need to know that the closed window is truth but that the open window is also truth. If you hope to perceive truth and existence in darkness, you must also see truth and existence in light. The question you should most care about involves not only the joy and propitiousness that people experience in the light together and the way they gasp and struggle in darkness, but also the anxiety they experience in the boundary zone between these two sets of windows.

THE UNREGULATED EXPANSION OF THE CENSORSHIP SYSTEM

When it comes to literature, a censorship system is like a cruel father admonishing his disobedient child. China's authors are as familiar with the nation's censorship system as a frequently beaten child knows the rules of his father's anger—and it is as though every author who has memory and experience knows the system as intimately as they know the palm of their own hand.

China's literary censorship system can be divided into three levels.

1   The national censorship system. For literary works, national censorship is a kind of ideological trial that involves a set of policies, rules, and regulations derived from ideology's service to the regime. Although all laws and regulations are determined by individuals, their start point and end point rely on the nation's reputation. Following a lengthy series of meetings and notifications, virtually every department and individual in contemporary China responsible for culture, news, literature, and art with ideological implications can consciously grasp censorship's policies and framework, its bottom line, and its outer margins. They understand what can and can't be written, what can be addressed in a vague fashion (like the Cultural Revolution) and what definitely cannot be mentioned at all (like June Fourth). However, what really leaves authors at a loss is the censorship operators: the individuals who implement specific cultural provisions on behalf of the Party.

2   Censorship operators. The censorship regime includes an array of different types of institutions that help implement literary policies. At the top level, these include the Central Propaganda Department, the General Administration of Press and Publication, and other high-level departments; at the middle level, they include provincial-level institutions; and at the bottom level, they include specific journals and presses. Regardless of how good or bad the policies may be, they all need operators in order to be carried out—the same way that after a law is passed, it needs judges in order to be implemented. The difference between laws and censorship policies is that although China's legal system is lax, the

laws themselves can be very strict, and for virtually any crime one can find a corresponding law—the same way that the law clearly specifies for how many years one can be imprisoned for robbery or rape. When it comes to censorship, however, it is not a question of matching an infraction to a legal provision, nor are there any defense lawyers to defend the accused or procurators to oversee the courts and judges. Instead, the entire system depends on the censorship operators' general conscience and their understanding of corresponding policies. These policies specify that literature cannot touch various devastating national and humanitarian tragedies brought about by the revolution—including the Anti-Rightist Campaign, the Great Leap Forward, the Great Iron-Smelting Campaign, the Great Famine, and the decade-long Cultural Revolution. Nevertheless, either out of a sense of artistic necessity or their own conscience, some authors have persisted in describing these tragedies. Because their works are ostensibly fictional and feature fictional characters, not to mention the fact that the significance of the works lies in their attention to literary art and human nature, many of them were ultimately published (today, of course, this would be utterly impossible). Strictly speaking, works like Wang Anyi's *Age of Enlightenment*, Jia Pingwa's *Old Kiln*, the first volume of Yu Hua's *Brothers*, Mo Yan's *Life and Death Are Wearing Me Out* and *Frog*, and my own *Hard Like Water* could all be considered to have touched on prohibited topics—although in the end they were all successfully published and were well-received. Meanwhile, some other works, such as Zhang Yihe's *The Past Is Not Like Smoke* and my own *Dream of Ding Village* and *The Four Books*, were either banned or were unable to be published in China. The divergent fates of these two sets of novels are the result of the censorship operators.

The ultimate determinant of how censorship is implemented is, of course, policy. Policy dictates what can and cannot be written, and when a work violates these policy restrictions, it will be seized and recalled. In practice, however, censorship operators—either because they seek promotion, because they are loyal to the Party, or because they are driven by emotion or a desire for power—often tighten a system that was originally designed to be flexible, leading to a significant intensification of the censorship process, like an elevator operator who transforms elevator buttons into a lock that will determine whether or not you will be able to return home.

Censorship is not merely censorship; it is also power. During many books' prolonged review process, authors must rely on their social connections (their *guanxi*) to ensure that their work will be approved. Meanwhile, other books are banned not strictly because of their subject matter but because of the temperament of the individual censors. It has been reported that Wei Hui and Mian Mian, while writing their novels *Shanghai Baby* and *Candy*, originally had an agreement whereby they would tell each other's stories, but later the two authors had a falling-out. When word of their original arrangement reached the censorship officials, the officials responded by banning both works and shutting down the entire publication process. This, in turn, set off a storm that left the presses' editors as silent as winter cicadas.

Two dominant characteristics of contemporary China's censorship system include the abuse of power, on one hand, and publishers' increased caution and expanded inspection, on the other. The first characteristic is shared by all Chinese departments (which typically consist of three parts power, seven parts expansion, and ten parts authoritarianism—this is power's necessary logic, and it also applies to specific publishing agencies, as well as newspaper, film, television, and other art groups). Publishers were originally the most direct implementers of the publishing industry and of grassroots culture, but now that censorship has become stricter and bans have become more and more common, censorship operators are increasingly required to attend not only to a work's subject matter but even to individual word use. As a result, it is very common for publishers and editors themselves to be examined, interrogated, suspended, and transferred.

Censorship operators frequently adopt a policy of punishing one author to serve as an example to others, on the logic that if you are bitten by a snake one morning, you will remain terrified of ropes for years to come. Accordingly, publishing organizations have become censorship operators on the principle that "all citizens are soldiers." After a manuscript arrives, the first thing editors consider is not the work's artistic or market value but whether it is sensitive and whether the author has attracted the attention of the higher-ups. In this way, editors become the book's first censors. The publisher's second-, third-, and final-round reviewers serve not only as the manuscript's artistic referees but also as its political censors. In the case of works that have artistic value but also carry a certain degree of risk, the publisher may extend the review process and allow the National Press and Publication Administration to make the final call.

3   Self-censorship. The national censorship system uses power and policies that outweigh the effects of law to call for the implementation and oversight of the censorship operation. Over time, however, this sort of operation ultimately succeeds in encouraging a process of self-censorship on the part of the authors themselves. If censorship operation is a kind of power and oppression, then authors' self-censorship is simultaneously conscious, unwitting, and reflexive.

Like many works, my own *Dream of Ding Village* underwent a process of self-censorship. I have already discussed this process at length elsewhere, but what I would like to add here relates to the conscious and reflexive nature of this process. The harm it causes is far greater than the processes of censorship, editing, and banning that people can see—because it involves literary elements that are excised before they are even born. Like a fetus that is subject to One-Child policy family-planning restrictions, these elements can disappear before they even have a chance to appear in the first place. Before they have even become a fetus, they are consciously and reflexively "planned" out of existence.

THE ADVANTAGES AND DISADVANTAGES OF THE PROFESSIONAL WRITERS' SYSTEM

China's professional writers' system is the most distinctive feature of the nation's socialist literature regime, in which power is used to standardize literature, thought, and art. This kind of administrative system is possible only in socialist countries, and it features the Chinese Writers' Association, which offers a means of nurturing and managing authors' thought, behavior, and writing (other art forms such as film, television, drama, painting, calligraphy, and folk art are overseen by the China Literature and Art Federation). The greatest advantage of the Chinese Writers' Association is that it ensures that many talented authors won't have to worry about basic living requirements and other practical considerations, and instead can devote themselves to their writing. Instead of a salon system, writers' associations use organizational and activity methods to discuss, pursue, and expand literature. However, because the basic objective of the professional author system is not artistic freedom and advancement but rather the management, regulation, and control of authors' writing, thought, and imagination, the potential advantages of the professional author system are mostly lost. There is only a minority of authors who, working within this collective system, manage to preserve the independence of their writing and their literary personality.

One of the greatest disadvantages of the professional author system is that it makes writers lazy and inclined to lose their creativity.

Because professional authors under this system are subject to a process of nationalization and politicization, they therefore receive the same compensation whether or not they actually work, and they achieve the same outcome whether or not they actually create anything. It has been thirty years since the beginning of the Reform and Opening Up Campaign, and the market economy is now society's most powerful force. However, professional authors can go for years without writing anything yet still draw a monthly salary from the Ministry of Treasury and Finance. This means that they could potentially write nothing at all and instead spend every day chatting, attending meetings, and participating in other activities. Many authors initially produce works bursting with talent when they start writing in their spare time, but their output decreases once they are incorporated into this professional author system. In fact, they may even stop writing altogether as they proceed to spend the rest of their life positioned as a professional author. The issue is not that those authors stop writing because they have become detached from reality and their feelings (or, as it is put in official discourse, because they have become detached from life), but rather that the professional writer system encourages people's inherent laziness, which in turn may dull their sensitivity, diligence, talent, and creativity.

The second disadvantage of the professional author system is that it encourages authors to lose their individuality and become collectivized and nationalized.

To tell the truth, writing is a very solitary and lonely endeavor vested with religious sentiment. However, the professional author system is essentially concerned with the collectivization, nationalization, and politicization of individual writing. The unification of thought, topics, and, when possible, artistic expression—all of this has the effect of collectivizing, politicizing, and nationalizing individual creation. From its initial publication, Mao Zedong's "Talks at the Yan'an Forum" has offered a model for China's policy on literature and art, and to this day it remains an important guide for ideology and for professional authors' writing, speech, and action. For several decades, there has been considerable study, discussion, and exploration of the origins of this speech and for whom it was intended, but essentially it sought to remove the religious sentiments that were in the service of the heart and soul. The text encouraged authors to abandon their individual religious sentiments and instead become members of a collective under a unified leadership and management. The result was to make literature eager to serve power and politics, as well as the Party and the Party's needs.

If, as an author, you hope to maintain a certain amount of stability in your life, you'll need to enter the ranks of professional authors. In doing so, your deep thought will have to undergo a process of collectivization, politicization, and nationalization. You'll have to recognize the regulations that policies and power apply to your writing, and how the publication process has, over the past several decades, cultivated readers' values. After recognizing all of this, you will transition from an individual into a collective and will complete (or potentially complete) literature's process of nationalization and collectivization. This is a basic but effective chain of survival, and it is also the system's most effective chain for managing thought. Once you become a link in this chain, your literary perspective, worldview, and even views on life and value will lose their independence and individuality, leaving you with a collective and national writing consciousness.

"Work within the system, but think outside the system." This saying captures an attitude held by many institutional staff and Chinese intellectuals. Many professional authors give lip service to this phrase, but very few adhere to it in their writing.

Works like Orwell's *Animal Farm* and Kafka's *The Trial* are not necessarily models that Chinese authors should pursue in their own writing. However, even in this bountiful land, authors' enlightened writing and artistic thought have been virtually eliminated. One must concede that for professional authors, method and form are indispensable and fruitful when it comes to the collectivization, politicization, and nationalization of their thought.

The third drawback of the professional author system is that it leads authors to lose their identity and independence—the same way that a company employee who draws a salary year after year must work on behalf of the company and express respect for his boss in his speech and actions. An author's job is to write, and his speech and actions are his work. Meanwhile, his company is the Chinese Writers' Association, and his bosses are political leaders and the Party that represents the people. This kind of system—in which I raise and educate you—is naturally for the purpose of having you work (write) for me. The system is not designed to encourage you to be independent, to be free, or to develop an unorthodox and unrestrained self-imagining.

To put it simply, the basic objective of the Chinese Writers' Association is to transform writers into Party authors. Before the Reform and Opening Up Campaign, all writers acknowledged and accepted the objective of becoming Party authors. Afterward, following writers' pursuit of artistic independence, the term *Party author* continued to be invoked in periodicals and at conferences, but it began to fade in many writers' hearts. Although the basic objective of the Chinese Writers' Association did not change, its methods did. From a compulsory and oppressive system, it shifted to one that emphasized education and inducements. It used traditional methods of meetings and study, together with a process of issuing awards and cultivating literary values, to achieve its objective of transforming authors into Party authors, together with an arrangement that emphasized the "freedom of pure art" and not a work's independent character.

The professional author system does not reject freedom of expression, but neither does it actively promote authors' independence. If you are in this system, the system allows you to be a writer who is not a Party author, but it does not permit you to produce writings that are neither "main melody" nor "positive energy" works. You can explore endlessly when it comes to your works' language and form, but this exploration cannot extend to the works' social content—including contemporary people, thought, soul, and sharp social contradictions. When it comes to artistic form, your thought can be independent, but when it comes to content, you are not allowed to think independently. If you disobey, your works will be rejected, censored, and derided, but if you obey, your works will be praised, promoted, and rewarded. In this way, a new standard for assessing literary value is established, as the objective of being a Party author or writing a Party work is replaced with that of producing a main melody or positive energy work. However, when virtually all authors decline to pursue the standard of main melody and positive energy works, while also trying their best to avoid the standard of negative energy works, their independence within this organization will be gradually weakened and even eliminated. In this way, the system will achieve its objective of managing authors.

Today, roughly 80 percent of Chinese authors who are middle-aged or older belong to these sorts of professional organizations. Young authors born in the eighties and nineties and new internet authors are rapidly being incorporated into this "unity" through membership in professional organizations such as the Chinese Writers' Association and other national organizations (including the National Congress of Writers and the National Congress of Young Creative Writers), the literary prize system (including the Mao Dun Prize and the Lu Xun Prize), and other means of honoring works. Through a process of assimilation, cultivation, and transformation, authors first become "a member of the team," then they gradually accept an assessment of literary value that is lacking in independent personality, and finally the system achieves its objective of having them produce works that lack independence, freedom, and thought.

A COPING MECHANISM WHEN WRITING UNDER EXTRAORDINARY CIRCUMSTANCES

Faced with China's current contradictory environment, which features a relatively open market economy and a relatively closed political system—an environment that is neither extreme left, like the Cultural Revolution, nor fully democratic, free, and balanced—authors have the possibility of enjoying independent thought and imagination, while also encountering enormous obstacles of identification and seduction. They have adopted a variety of different responses to this predicament.

One response has been to behave submissively, focus on profitable writing, and treat literary talent as a condition for honor, status, and profit. This kind of response is very common among Chinese authors, for whom existence and life become the best rationale for an exchange wherein authors take the position: "I'll do my best on behalf of your main melody and positive energy, if in return you help improve my life by offering me cars, houses, reimbursement slips, prizes, and official positions" (positions like the director or deputy director of China's various writers' associations). The Chinese people have always contended that food is an issue of paramount importance, and as soon as literature and life are united, all writing for the purpose of flattery, supremacy, material benefit, and honor becomes reasonable and legitimate, while also enjoying an unquestionable legitimacy. This is a position taken by many contemporary authors.

A second possible response has been to escape, resulting in a literature that is very deserving of respect. "Everything I do is for the sake of literature itself" — this attitude involves reducing literature to a kind of ivory tower, or using the ivory tower's reputation to distance oneself from the chaos of power, mainstream culture, and social complexity. In this way, one can sit alone in one's study or stroll through the peach blossom garden, using writing as a home and Zhuangzi's withdrawal as a basis while enjoying a peaceful life and writing process. Even if one is not in one's study or garden every day, and even if one enters secular life and social reality every day, one's writing may still be characterized by a pattern of avoidance, escape, and a pursuit of "purity." This is not merely an attitude; it is also a method and an entire worldview. It is a kind of position and response for contemporary Chinese authors who possess thought, goals, and talent. It is also precisely the distanced diligent quality of these works that enriches the existence and status of contemporary Chinese literature. At the level of their personality there is perhaps not much "I think, therefore I am" independence, but these authors have independent goals and qualities in their writing. They represent Chinese literature's nucleus and mainstay while also maintaining its future prospects.

A third response has been adopted by writers who hope to preserve independent thought in their literature while at the same time maintaining their status as independent authors. These authors dare to confront humanity's predicament and reality, to confront writing, and to confront literature's existence in contemporary reality, while also daring to confront the existence of people and reality within literature. These writers do not seek to become independent by adopting the attitude of a challenger, and instead they use their identity as authors to stand beside or in front of reality while observing and reflecting on everything within that same reality. Without attempting to avoid anything, they instead display the greatest possible concern and love for contemporary China's absurd, complex, and surging existence, as well as for the contemporary predicament in which people find themselves. They don't imagine that literature will change anything overnight, but instead they focus on what literature might leave in this gap between history and the present. Their literature speaks not only to the present but also to life and to the world.

Among the most important Chinese works from recent years that examine reality we could cite Jia Pingwa's *Qin Opera* and *Old Kiln*, Wang Anyi's *Age of Enlightenment*, Mo Yan's *Life and Death Are Wearing Me Out* and *Frog*, Yu Hua's *Brothers*, Liu Zhenyun's *Someone to Talk To*, Su Tong's *The Boat to Redemption*, Ge Fei's *Spring Comes to the South*, together with several more recent works that I read as I was preparing this manuscript, including Han Shaogong's *Book of Day and Night*, Su Tong's *Shadow of the Hunter*, Jia Pingwa's *The Lantern Bearer*, and Yu Hua's *The Seventh Day*. Although these are not necessarily the most representative works of Chinese literature, or even of the oeuvre of these individual authors, each work nevertheless illustrates how its author abandoned a distanced attitude to focus instead on history and contemporary reality, and on the people who cannot avoid contemporary society's absurdities. This clearly demonstrates that what these authors are pursuing is not only artistic completeness but also the independence of the authors' personality.

The independence and completeness of the authors' personality does not mark the arrival of a great era of true literature, but at least it foretells Chinese literature's possible rise.

8   Fear and Betrayal Have Accompanied Me throughout My Life

This is a topic that is not particularly happy or light. However, here I open the innermost region of my heart not so that others may share it, but rather so that they may at least understand it.

More specifically, the topic I'd like to discuss is how fear and betrayal have accompanied me throughout my life.

WHAT DO I FEAR?

First, I fear power.

I was never a brave child. Once, when I was four or five, I saw a wolf standing in front of our house. It appeared emaciated, famished, and dingy. At the time our family lived at the entrance to the village, so when I opened the door and saw the animal standing there, I stared back in shock. I initially thought it was just a hungry dog and wanted to go find something for it to eat, but in the end we simply stared at each other. Because during that period I myself never had enough to eat and was always hungry, I therefore had nothing to feed the animal. So we both just stood there staring at each other. Eventually, another villager came over and shooed the animal away, and it was only then that I realized it was a wolf. The other villager shouted at me, "A little longer and that wolf would have eaten you!" From that point on, I've felt a strange love and fear of wolves. That wolf was hungry and emaciated, and it could have devoured me at any time. However, its eyes were filled with a warm, pleading glow.

I once remarked that ever since I was a child, I've had three idols: the city, power, and health. Today, these can be understood as follows: (1) the city is modern civilization, (2) power is a force that controls your fate, and (3) health is life. Of these three idols, the first to be transformed into fear was power. The fear I currently feel in the face of power is like that which I felt toward that wolf. It is amorphous yet ubiquitous. It can bring you prestige, money, fame, and anything else you might desire, but it can also bring you death, alter your fate, and transform you from a millionaire into a pauper or from an angel into a devil.

When I was young, hunger followed me around like a dog's tail. Every day on my way to and from school, I could see the township cadres—although at the time they were known as people's commune cadres. At mealtime, with their water bottle in hand and their spoon knocking against their enamel bowl, they would go to the canteen to enjoy meat dishes and steamed buns. Why was it that everyone else in the village and surrounding areas lacked even coarse grain, yet these cadres could enjoy meat dishes and steamed buns? It is because they, as national cadres, had power. From that point on, I cultivated an ideal of being able to escape from the countryside and seek my fortune—hoping that one day I might become a national cadre with a monthly salary, with abundant food, dignity, and a reputation!

When I was twenty, I joined the army and took the first step toward changing my fate. Although I had already begun to write before joining the army, at the time it was not because I wanted to become an author but rather because I hoped to use writing to change my fate—to ensure that I had enough to eat and drink, and to help become either a city dweller or someone with power (like a village head). Later, I did in fact achieve some distinction through my writing. I was promoted to cadre and became not only a city dweller but also someone who held a certain amount of power.

The first time I realized I held a modicum of power was during a couple of incidents following my promotion to platoon leader when I was twenty-five and then to political instructor when I was twenty-six. First, I went to report to another military company one afternoon, and that night when I went to bed, I discovered that our unit's communications officer had already put toothpaste on my toothbrush, placed my foot-washing basin next to my bed, and hung a towel for drying my feet on the back of a chair. When the baby-faced communications officer smiled at me politely, a strange feeling of sorrow welled up from the bottom of my heart. It was as if I were seeing my own son or younger brother working as a servant for a bowl of food. Of course, it is an exquisite feeling when someone prepares your toothpaste for you and brings you your foot-washing basin: this means you have become an official and now possess power.

However, it was during an incident on my second day as political instructor that I realized even more clearly that I had truly become an official and held power. At six that morning, I led our troops out for a run, and at seven we returned, dripping in sweat. When I entered my room to change my shoes, I pulled back the bedsheets and saw that a soldier had placed a tea set under my bed. There was also a satin cloth next to my pillow and a bottle of liquor and a cigarette on the table facing the window.

This was in 1985, and the people who had brought me these gifts were soldiers seeking to curry favor—given that I was a leading figure in the military company. If they weren't seeking vacation time to return home, they were attempting to join the Party or have a sanction removed from their official file. For assorted reasons, nearly thirty of the hundred or so troops in our company—which amounts to a quarter of the company—had warnings or sanctions in their files. At that time, soldiers with sanctions in their files would not be able to find work after they left the army. This was the situation in the company where I was stationed, and this was also the first time I realized that power was not merely power, but rather it was a magic wand capable of controlling other people's lives.

From that point on, I developed a fascination with and a fear of power. I think that the most commendable thing I did that year was to take all the gifts the soldiers had given me and return them. At the same time, I also granted all the requests I received, which almost without exception were entirely reasonable. Of the soldiers who wanted to advance their careers, nearly all were accepted into the Party—although I'm not sure whether this ultimately ended up helping them or harming them. Of those who wanted to return home to visit their parents or grandparents,

I secretly gave them all a few days off. And of the nearly thirty soldiers who had sanctions in their files, I secretly arranged for the sanctions to be removed as long as they continued to perform well—thereby leaving them with a clean slate so that they could continue to train and work.

As a result, within half a year our company, which had previously been the worst in the division, had been completely transformed. To describe the result using a popular slogan, this was a case of "giving an old look a new face." Nevertheless, I also recognized that the company's remarkable transformation was a result not of my wisdom, but rather of my power. For instance, when soldiers requested time off to return home, the camp ordinarily had to agree and report to the military group for arrangements. I, however, didn't need to notify anyone and instead could use my own authority to allow the soldiers to return home. Similarly, for a soldier in good standing to have a sanction removed from his file, the company branch would ordinarily have to research the issue and reach a decision, and then report to the camp for approval. I, however, didn't need to tell anyone and instead could make the decision on my own.

At the end of that year, the division recognized me as an outstanding grassroots cadre.

The following year, I was appointed to serve as the army's propaganda officer. As I was leaving my military company, the other soldiers broke into tears and couldn't bear to see me go. However, I knew very well that my emotional connection with them was grounded entirely on my use and abuse of power. Because those twenty or so soldiers from throughout China no longer had any disciplinary sanctions in their files, they were able to secure good jobs when they retired from the army, thereby enabling them to have a new start on their new career, future marriage, and family. All of this was not because of me, but rather it was because of power, combined with my ability, as a low-level political instructor, to use and abuse that power.

Later, the situation was not as ideal, and many things underwent terrifying changes. Of these, the most unforgettable was one time when, for some reason, I left the military camp to have a meal with an official, and we were joined by the leader of the local public security bureau and his chauffeur. In China, chauffeurs don't usually eat at the same table as leaders, but given that there were not many of us present that day, the bureau director let the chauffeur dine with us. The problem was that ordinarily the chauffeur should have left the table to wait outside as soon as he finished eating, but given that everyone was recounting enthralling stories and telling jokes that were so hilarious that we collapsed in paroxysms of laughter, the young chauffeur decided to stick around. As the senior official and the bureau director laughed heartily, they became increasingly relaxed, but when their jokes shifted to more raunchy topics, they suddenly realized that there was an "outsider" sitting at the table with them. This outsider was, of course, the chauffeur. Ordinarily, a chauffeur should not be privy to leaders' conversation, but because our conversation was so entertaining, our chauffer was still sitting there, having completely forgotten that he was supposed to leave after he finished eating. When the official was about to reach the climax of his joke, he noticed the chauffeur sitting across from him, whereupon he paused and stared.

Realizing his mistake, the chauffeur promptly got up and left.

The bureau director looked apologetically at the official, and said, "I'm sorry."

The official replied, "It's OK. Just be sure to discipline him."

With this, the incident passed.

At least I thought it had passed, the way that drizzle is dried up by the sun. When I returned from the office the following afternoon, however, I found the chauffeur waiting for me. I don't know how he was able to find my house, but he was squatting by the side of the road like a heartbroken child. When he saw me, he approached and explained that he had just been dismissed from his job because he had heard too much at the previous day's dinner. He hoped I might go talk to his former boss and request that he contact the bureau official and request that the chauffeur be allowed to keep his job. The chauffeur said that he had used all sorts of *guanxi* (connections) to obtain his job and that his family was very proud that he worked for the director of the public security bureau. Furthermore, his entire family relied on his income, but now that he had been dismissed, he no longer had a job.

I was stunned.

I agreed to go speak to the official.

When I went to work the next day, I proceeded to the official's office and explained what had happened to the chauffeur, adding that I thought he was very unfortunate. I asked if the official could call the bureau director and request that the chauffeur be allowed to keep his job.

When I concluded, the official simply gazed at me. After a long silence, he asked, "Do you feel that so-and-so (the public security bureau director) did anything wrong?"

I was dumbfounded.

The official continued. "I never expected that so-and-so would be so capable and efficient. If he were in the army, he would definitely be someone who could lead soldiers into battle!"

I was speechless. I literally didn't utter a single word. Eventually, realizing it was pointless to stay, I left.

As a result, the chauffeur did in fact lose his job.

This is power. This is the fear that exists because of power!

Power contains a magical force capable of casually transforming people and their fate. Some people find this magical force entrancing, but others find it utterly terrifying!

My fear of power may very well have begun from that incident with the chauffeur. Afterward, countless other developments led my attitude to shift from reverence to awe, and finally to bona fide terror. My fear of power was born at that time, and it quickly became rooted in my brain. From that point on, I shifted my focus from trying to get promoted to pursuing literature. I began revising my life and goals, and became convinced that my life belonged to literature, even if literature didn't necessarily belong to me.

In 1994 I was transferred to a new military unit in Beijing, where everyone treated me very well. While I was there, however, I suffered a herniated disc and sought treatment at countless different clinics, but to no avail. It eventually got to the point that I couldn't walk, much less carry anything. I completed all my works from that period, including *The Years, Months, Days* and *Streams of Time*, while either lying flat in bed or else sitting in a recliner designed specifically for handicapped people. At that time, I learned that the Ji'nan military zone in Shandong had developed a new treatment for this sort of injury, so I went there for an operation. Just as I was about to enter the operating room, however, I received a phone call from the leader of my military unit in Beijing telling me to return immediately.

I replied that I was about to have surgery.

The leader said that there had been an emergency, and even if I was already lying on the operating table, I needed to get down and return home immediately.

That same day, my wife and I rushed back to Beijing, where I learned that my novel *Summer Sunset* had been critiqued in an article, resulting in its being censored. Beginning at that moment and for nearly half a year, I lay in bed and wrote one self-criticism after another, but none were accepted. By that point I had already arranged for my wife and son to return to my family home and work the land, thinking that if my self-criticisms weren't going to be accepted, I would stop writing them and give up trying to reform myself. However, one day my military unit's highest official came over with a bag of fruit. He informed me that my issue had been resolved and that in the future I should simply write more works praising the military, the nation, and heroes. As the official was telling me this, my eyes filled with tears of gratitude, and after he left, I immediately began sobbing. I was of course grateful that my fate had been rectified, but I also felt an inexplicable and sourceless fear of power. It was as though someone were walking alone through the quiet night, surrounded by empty wilderness and bright moonlight as peaceful as water. It was so quiet that it seemed I could hear the moonlight falling to Earth, which terrified me to the point that I immediately wanted to turn and run away.

I began using literature to flee, and resolved that from that point on I would no longer write about military topics. This is because in works on military topics, the reality I see, feel, and experience is different from that of other people. It is also because I yearned to use my individual style to express what I perceive and know about the interpersonal relations and the world I inhabit. Because I have a natural fear of power, I decided to focus on literature. However, given that writing military fiction could lead to my being oppressed by power, I decided to devote myself instead to writing about rural topics. In the following years, I wrote the novels *Streams of Time*, *Hard Like Water*, and *Lenin's Kisses*, together with some allegorical rural-themed novellas and short stories. However, one evening not long after the publication of *Lenin's Kisses*, and just as I was thinking I had opened a new direction in my literature, Hong Kong's Phoenix TV broadcast an interview with me. The interview aired at eight in the evening, and at eight the next morning the leader of my army unit called me up at home and said, "The senior officials all watched your interview on Phoenix TV last night and feel that you should leave the army."

A few minutes later, and before I had fully processed what had just happened, an official from the army's employment transfer office called me to say that I had three days to find another job. He added that if I was unable to find a job within three days, I would have to accept the new position that the organization assigned me, which might well be in Changping—one of Beijing's outer suburbs, extremely far from the city center. I entreated this official—but in reality, I was entreating power itself—that I instead be reassigned to my original hometown. This was the countryside I originally left and to which I wanted to return.

The official replied, "You are a cadre and must accept the organization's assignment. You shouldn't make requests of the organization."

And thus, in the blink of an eye, I was kicked out of the army.

It was only afterward that I learned that a lieutenant general who liked to read had just been transferred into our unit. One day he mentioned he had recently read two books, one of which was *Lenin's Kisses* and the other was Zhang Yihe's *The Past Is Not Like Smoke* (which was later banned). He remarked that if China were to have another Anti-Rightist Campaign and was given a quota of only two targets to persecute, the authors of these two novels should be used to fill that quota. When this lieutenant general heard me joke on Phoenix Television that "authors are like decorative flower vases, and sometimes leaders will ask you to join them for a meal. Even if you repeatedly offer toasts while at the table, the leader won't necessarily remember you, but if you *don't* offer a toast, he will definitely remember you forever." It appears that this joke was the fuse that led to my being kicked out of the army. Therefore, when I came to work the next morning, the first thing the officials did was notify me that I had to immediately leave the army unit where I had lived, worked, and written for twenty-six years. Power is an enormous magic wand full of pride, evil, and sinister force; when it is benevolent, it can grant you lots of money and fresh flowers, but if it is even slightly angered, your fate and your entire family's fate may become like a line of ants blown away by a capricious gust of wind.

Of course, I don't think that my fate is any more unbearable than that of other Chinese. A few years ago, after you made a considerable effort to purchase a house in Beijing, power ordered that the building be demolished, and decreed that if you didn't cooperate, police would appear at your door. Furthermore, your house would be robbed and have its electricity and water cut off, and it would have stones thrown through its windows. When you went to complain to the national cadres at the demolition office, they replied mockingly, "Go ahead and report this. The doors to the courthouse are always open!" This is how power makes you understand that your life is worth less than that of a pig or a dog. When a pig is threatened, it will resist and rush at you, and when a dog is threatened, it will attack and bite you. When it comes to people, however, our dignity as humans under power is comparable to ants and mosquitoes. We don't even have as much courage to resist as dogs and pigs. Where we differ from these animals, however, is that we are sensitive, are fragile, and have memory. An injury—even if it is not very serious—can leave us with lifelong pain.

Therefore, fear accompanies you throughout your life.

Fear becomes a lifelong companion that accompanies you even more closely than your wife, son, or parents. It becomes your skin and hair, and eventually it becomes your blood and internal organs. It becomes a caution in dealing with others and cannot help but become your general worldview. Because this revises and changes your literary perspective, it becomes the start point and end point of all your writing.

However, when it comes to the relationship between fear and life, fate and writing, the fear of power is only one element, and it is not even the most sensitive and unforgettable one.

What I find most difficult to discuss is my fear of death and my corresponding worship of health and longevity. Dating back to when I was just a few years old, whenever I think of death I invariably end up being unable to sleep all night. I frequently burst into tears and feel that life is meaningless. I fear death and am terrified of the end, and I find myself in agony every hour of every day. I attempt to avoid this fear through a process of ignoring and forgetting.

Because people fear death, they become determined to live and are even more inclined to worship health and longevity. They feel that even if life is meaningless, they still want to live. Meanwhile, you may become bored with family and daily life, and this boredom may develop into fear—a new fear that appears to come out of nowhere. In this way, power, death, family, and ordinariness become a net that surrounds you—and you are a bird caught in this net of fear, a blade of grass in a wasteland of fear, a fallen leaf and drop of water in a forest of fear. You write for the sake of the desolation of this countryside of fear, but in the end your writing leads you to view the contemporary world with an even greater sense of fear, desolation, and unease. This is the start point, process, and end point of your writing.

You begin with fear, pass by fear, and end up in fear.

THE REAL WORLD IS MY SPIRITUAL CONCENTRATION CAMP

How can a cowardly and fearful person adopt a tough posture in his writing?

Based only on my writing, no one would guess that I am a nervous and fearful person, and some might assume that I am a hard and rough—and even brave and resistant—writer. That may be how things are, but when I say "how things are," I am not referring to the phenomenon whereby authors lack something in real life but try to compensate for it in their writing, or where they fill their writing with what they can't enjoy in real life. Instead, I flee because of fear, and because I flee, I therefore betray. It is only through my writing that I can display a tough artistic resistance.

Because of the rural poverty you experienced when you were young, you therefore became sensitive and fearful—and ever since, a desire to escape poverty has remained buried in your heart. After you finally succeeded in escaping, you may have looked back at your earlier life with a sense of nostalgia, but in the end what became dominant was your escape and betrayal of that kind of life—this being the main melody of your life at that time. Similarly, because there is love, there is also hatred—leading to the paradox whereby the sharper your hatred, the deeper your love. In real life, if you loathe or fear something, you will automatically resist and oppose it, but when you lack the ability to resist something directly, escape may become your primary means of resistance. Meanwhile, after you succeed in escaping, it becomes necessary for you to betray.

In reality, I am the kind of person who uses escape as a form of resistance. After I began writing literature, however, this kind of escape became a kind of betrayal, whereupon I became someone who uses literature to betray reality. Many people claim that my writing reflects the filial love of a son of the soil, but I believe I am actually an *unfilial* son of the soil—a real-life traitor. In life, my disgust with and fear of rural life led me to try to escape, but after escaping I didn't have the same sense of attachment to the soil that other people do. Therefore, unlike Shen Congwen, I don't write works that are full of beauty and love for the soil and the distant countryside, or at least I haven't yet written any. Instead, I have inherited Lu Xun's feelings of nostalgia, gloom, and critique for the countryside. I'm not sure why the drops of tenderness toward the countryside that appeared in my early works later decreased and why as I gradually gained a greater familiarity with contemporary life, they eventually disappeared altogether. In my oeuvre, works like *Streams of Time, Hard Like Water, Dream of Ding Village, The Four Books, The Explosion Chronicles,* and *Ballad, Hymn, Ode* all feature an examination and betrayal of the land, and could even be viewed as a kind of interrogation and trial. Sometimes I recognize that this approach cannot avoid being simple and repetitive, but after I enter the writing process I no longer have that sort of tender love.

In China some authors claim they write for the common people, whereas others claim they speak on behalf of the subaltern. Some say their writing has a downward gaze (like literature by so-called sent-down youths), others say theirs has an upward gaze, and still others say theirs has a level gaze, meaning that it is positioned on the same plane as life itself. As for my own writing, although some people may claim that it has a level gaze and others may claim that it has an upward gaze, I myself feel that I escaped from life and am now a bystander—like someone who escapes from a spiritual concentration camp and then observes, remembers, and inspects the camp's detainees and incidents.

Real life is your spiritual concentration camp, and writing is the terrifying process of recollection and recounting after escaping from the camp. Because you view life like a former detainee, your position and posture as a writer will naturally not be tolerated by contemporary reality. That is why *Hard Like Water* was deemed to be "transgressive with respect to both red [revolution] and yellow [sex]," meaning that controversy was inevitable. *Lenin's Kisses* became a convenient excuse for power to kick you out of the army. After you left the army, where power is most concentrated, you assumed that you would no longer feel so oppressed that you couldn't even breathe. You assumed that you would experience an unprecedented sense of freedom and would enjoy a feeling of liberation as though it had suddenly dropped from the sky. When this sense of real-life liberation is transmitted into literature, it approximates the kind of free and casual nonsense that one finds in *Serve the People!* However, *Serve the People!* aroused considerable controversy in China, where it was critiqued, banned, and "discussed," which in turn influenced your own life.

Let me share an anecdote. When *Serve the People!* was initially banned, the notification was distributed overnight to propaganda departments around the country. Although by that point I had already left the army, I was still living in an army residential district and initially had no idea what had just befallen the novel. The sun was still shining brightly in the sky, and flowers were blooming in the warm spring weather, but when I emerged from my residence the next day, I found that all my former colleagues were giving me the cold shoulder. Whenever they saw me approaching, they tried to avoid me like the plague, and when my wife went shopping for groceries, she found that our neighbors wouldn't even greet her in the street. It was only several days later that I learned that *Serve the People!* had been banned in response to a secret document from the central authorities and an emergency notification distributed by the army. At that point I had already left the army, but when the document was circulated, army officials were still told that "no one may have any interaction with Yan Lianke."

In this way, I became an enemy—a monster whom people had to avoid. Because my writing brought trouble to my new work unit, I felt I owed them an enormous debt. Meanwhile, the journal that published *Serve the People!* was sanctioned, fined, and reviewed. It was as though virtually every colleague at the journal had come from an enemy-occupied area and consequently couldn't be trusted. They all had to undergo a rigorous review process before they could secure a figurative customs clearance.

Because my fear of real life led me to escape into my fiction, being this literary "North Korean defector" became a greater source of fear in my life. A few days ago, I happened to mention *Dream of Ding Village* to someone. That work was my attempt to compromise with cruel reality—an attempt to "bow my head and compromise" in the face of power and fear. Within my overall oeuvre, *Dream of Ding Village* was a spiritual journey full of human warmth. However, I don't know whether it was because the higher-ups could not appreciate this novel's approach or because the author had already come to be perceived as a "North Korean defector" who could not be trusted, but just three days after the novel was published, printing was halted and the book was banned. From this point on, the author became a symbol of someone who could not be trusted. Every one of his works was subjected to special consideration by editors and publishers, as well as higher departmental officials and even the publishing administration. In real life, he basically became a heretical and dissenting figure, and it was as though every word and phrase that appeared in his writings was assumed to have ulterior motives.

You are a professional author, but when none of your writings could be trusted, and when even the republication of an old essay collection was singled out by the publishing administration for special consideration, you found yourself in a state of constant anxiety. Moreover, this anxiety then became your writing and your life. It became not only your spiritual existence but also your real life. When you are eating, you can obviously distinguish between your pen and your chopsticks, but when you are writing you find you are unable to differentiate between your life on paper and your spiritual or daily life.

In this way, fear became part of your daily existence, the same way that writing became part of your life. As long as you are alive, you must continue to write, and if you write, you will necessarily be anxious and fearful. Because of your fear and your attempts to flee that fear, in your writings you may adopt an attitude of "I'm not afraid of you"—the same way a child wandering through the wilderness may repeatedly cry out "I'm not scared! I'm not scared!" He shouts "I'm not scared" precisely because he is afraid, although in doing so he becomes even more afraid.

I face my reality like someone facing their spiritual concentration camp. Meanwhile, my writing is like a timid child who, in his terror, repeatedly shouts "I'm not scared, I'm not scared!" This is my greatest fear and trepidation.

I CRY EVERY DAY

For the past few years, I've been writing nonstop. Regardless of how poor my health might be, I write virtually every day that I'm home. I've written essays and novels, as well as works of literary criticism. However, what I would really like to write is a book that would be titled *Why I*

Want to Cry Every Day. This would not be a work of fiction but rather a "documentary of emotion." I can't say what precisely this book would document or what exactly I would write. When the idea for this book first occurred to me several years ago, I wanted to immediately go write it. After being sown in my heart, the seed took root and sprouted, and although it is not clear when it will flower and bear fruit, it nevertheless continues sprouting branches and vines month after month, year after year.

I must acknowledge that I am not particularly manly. This is probably not something that an author who has even a trace of masculinity should admit, but I am perhaps the world's least accomplished man. Often when I am alone, I'll think of something that makes me burst out crying, and I'll sob silently until my face is soaked in tears. For instance, about three years ago I was sitting at my window gazing down at a pagoda, and I'm not sure what I was thinking—maybe Buddhism made me think of death—but I suddenly began bawling. I sat alone on the floor, sobbing like an orphaned child. I wept and wept until I was exhausted and went to bed, but even in bed I soaked my pillowcase in tears.

On another occasion, my wife and I once quarreled over some minor matter, after which she asked what I wanted for lunch and then went out to buy some groceries. After she left, I immediately burst into tears. When she returned and noticed my bloodshot eyes, she asked why I was crying, and it was only then that I stopped. Why *was* I crying? I don't know; I really don't! I simply felt that life was meaningless, like a concentration camp full of anxiety, fear, and hopelessness. However, at the thought of death and corporeal liberation, I felt as though fear and hopelessness were life itself, and anxiety was a necessary part of existence. There was nothing for me to say, as I silently acquiesced to everything. My silence toward fate became a fundamental part of fate itself, just as my helplessness toward reality became a fundamental part of life itself. Writing, meanwhile, became the only meaningful thing in your life.

Although I never believed I would be able to write as well as others, I nevertheless had to keep writing day after day.

I never really understood the meaning of my writing during the latter half of my life. Although I recognize that my early work was for the purpose of escaping the land and resisting my fate, I'm unclear as to the significance of my later work. Nevertheless, I have no choice but to continue writing—word by word, line by line, and work by work. I have no choice but to write, although I don't know why I do so. The world resembles my spiritual concentration camp, and even as my writings scrutinize, resent, and criticize that reality, they also contain a layer of love—like a recently released prisoner who remains nostalgic for prison life. I don't know why this is. The one thing I do know is that when I am writing—when I'm facing a sheet of paper with pen in hand—I inevitably feel I am a living person, a living person with a certain degree of dignity.

I was at Hong Kong Baptist University last April, and because I write by hand, I could go for days without even opening my computer. One day, however, I received a call from Beijing saying that my in-box contained an email from so-and-so in the United States and that I should consider this carefully. After receiving this call, I endured several sleepless nights during which I would repeatedly get in the middle of the night to read and write until finally, exhausted, I'd return to bed. After my house was forcibly demolished, someone suggested that the public security bureau had already entered my life and investigated my past. They said I should keep my mouth shut and stop writing. Therefore, I sat anxiously in my room and didn't dare go outside to discuss my experience with the demolition. I didn't even dare post about it on Weibo. I was as helpless as a lost lamb unable to find its way home, and as fearful as a helpless dog. I hated my weakness and cowardice. My literati integrity was like a blade of grass that could be toppled by the slightest breath of wind, and I knew very well what I could and couldn't do.

Although I was fearful and anxious in real life, I used my writing to escape, escape, escape. Writing became my refuge. My fiction was not a direct reflection of reality, and instead it was the site of my internal escape. I used different ways of telling stories and told different kinds of stories. In this way, I used my writing to flee, even as this flight revealed a certain kind of resistance and betrayal. It was as if I resisted because I fled, and I betrayed because I resisted. It was precisely because I betrayed that I became even more involved. This was the vicious cycle that developed between my writing and my life. In the end, although my life was not reduceable to my writing, my writing was my life. Although my life will not necessarily influence my fate, writing must be my fate.

Because of this circular logic, when reality becomes your spiritual concentration camp and you don't have the ability to resist directly, you may instead use your writing to flee or betray. You attempt to use your novels to liberate yourself from your weakness of reality, as your writing naturally heads from escape to betrayal—heading toward what appears to be the greatest independence, as you thereby become a traitor to writing. The term *traitor* here refers not only to the novels' content, plot, and characters but also to artistic elements such as narrative style, language use, structural techniques, and the literary views and worldviews contained within the literary work. These elements gradually disappear into the distance like a runaway horse, heading in a direction in which they may be even more misread and misunderstood. Like *The Four Books* and my recently completed *The Explosion Chronicles*, these elements flee from—and simultaneously betray—the reality of contemporary China, even as they also use this flight and betrayal to directly intervene with reality. In the novels' artistic thinking, flight and betrayal help realize a new order within Chinese fiction, though not one that those readers and critics who are collective, intrinsic, and included in government structures would be able to recognize and accept. As a result, *The Four Books* could not be published in China, and the fate of *The Explosion Chronicles* currently remains uncertain.

In finding that you are unable to publish in your native language and in your home country the works you would most like for readers to read, you experience the desolation of having your soul being exiled to a distant site. You appreciate how wise it was to drive dissidents out of the country, like sending a boxer out of the ring to an empty area where he can box against empty air. Meanwhile, by exiling a novel that—in its content and form, its thought and imagination—is inclined toward betrayal, this permits you to live and permits your spirit to wander abroad. It allows your life to be grounded while also leaving you with a disorienting floating feeling.

It must be acknowledged that this kind of floating feeling is far gentler and more practical than having your flesh and soul wander in exile far from the territory of your native language. But sometimes, and for some people, this kind of grounded floating sensation leaves you feeling more anxious and fearful than if you were in exile abroad. From a certain perspective, to be completely in exile is also a form of complete liberation and a new beginning. But if you are constantly standing on the land of your native language while letting your writing—your spirit and soul—go into exile, this leaves you unable to enjoy a kind of completeness, and instead it can have only a sense of yearning. You cannot attain complete self-independence, and instead you can retain only a sort of stubbornness within weakness. Therefore, uneasiness and fear arrive, as the real world becomes your spiritual concentration camp. Meanwhile, writing, because it is unable to liberate your spirit, can give your spirit only a sense of floating while wandering in exile, and cannot help it truly escape. But other than write, what else can we do? Without writing, we have nothing. Nevertheless, it is difficult for writing to rescue itself. People who cannot put down their pen have no choice but to continue writing, and if they continue writing, the possibility of fear, unease, anxiety, and betrayal will remain forever entangled with them and will accompany them their entire life.

9 Writing under a Sky of Concentrated Power and Relative Laxity

Let us imagine the following scenario.

A captive tiger escapes and cannot be returned to its cage, at which point its keeper is faced with the following three options. First, the keeper may shoot and kill the tiger, but then he would lose his job and be sent home. Second, the tiger may be allowed to return to being king of the mountain, enjoying the company of the forests, rivers, and sky, and once again become a son of nature. Under this second option, however, the keeper would still end up unemployed, and although the tiger would be completed, the keeper would have to sacrifice his career, his power, and the dignity he derives from the awe of the spectators. In the end, the keeper would let the tiger return to the mountains while he himself would have to go back to working in the fields. Third, if the keeper is unable to recapture the tiger and put it back in its cage but is also unwilling to let it return to the wild, the best solution may be to simply provide the tiger with a piece of land that resembles its original environment, where it could roam freely within a certain range while eating fresh meat provided by the keeper. That way, the tiger would enjoy a limited amount of freedom and would not be as motivated to try to regain its truly free life in the wild. Meanwhile, because the keeper has the fresh meat the tiger needs, the tiger wouldn't stray far, but neither would it need to be caged (which would also mean that the keeper wouldn't risk injury when entering the cage to feed the animal). Meanwhile, the keeper would retain his job, his career, his salary, as well as the satisfaction he derives from feeding and caring for the tiger, while also maintaining his majesty, his power, and the dignity he derives from the awe of the spectators.

Accordingly, it appears that after the tiger escapes its cage, the third arrangement would offer the best tiger-human relationship.

Under this third arrangement, the tiger would be simultaneously free and captive, which is also the special relationship that exists between contemporary China's politics and its market economy, as well as between the nation's Chinese-style centralized power and its literature. Unfortunately, however, Chinese literature is not a beautiful tiger but rather a relatively docile sheep.

AN ECONOMIC ZONE AT THE INTERSTICES OF HAZE AND SUNSHINE

There are some topics relating to Chinese literature that one cannot avoid, the same way that a ship cannot leave the ocean and a car cannot stray from the road. For instance, it may be possible for literature to avoid politics, but for an author to avoid politics is as futile as trying to avoid the plague—given that politics can always come knocking in the middle of the night, take up residence in your living room, and become impossible to ignore.

Given that in China no literary work can truly escape the attention of the censorship system, how can any author claim that his or her works are independent of politics? Of course, in discussing how Chinese authors—like authors around the world—shudder at the mention of politics and power, we should also specify that contemporary Chinese-style politics is distinct from the absolute power that we had in China under Mao more than three decades ago or that you currently find in North Korea. The biggest difference involves the contrast between the open nature of contemporary China's economy and the closed nature of its politics. In this tension between openness and closure, the market economy is like the tiger released from its cage—and given that it may not be possible to truly return the animal to its cage and close the gate, one may therefore have no option but to offer it a relatively open sky and free territory. Then the tiger would resemble a car that must follow an existing road rather than a ship that can sail freely in any direction. You would just need to give the tiger—which is to say, the market economy and people's speech and thought—a relative amount of freedom, to permit the economy to breathe and let people speak and think without restraint. In this way they could gasp and struggle within the fissures of power. The relationship between China's politics and economy would resemble the relationship between the freed tiger and the keeper's fresh meat—and if politics does not offer the economy a modicum of freedom and nourishment, then when the economy becomes hungry, it may injure people and even topple the pedestals of power. However, if you give the economy too much space, then when it rushes toward the freedom that is rightfully its own, it may in the process pull down the seat of power.

The relationship between centralized power and relative laxity derives from the relationship between Chinese-style politics and China's market economy. Under one kind of democratic system, if you let the mountains, rivers, and the tiger return to their natural state, they will have their own distinctive characteristics while also belonging to nature. So-called freedom and harmony are really concerned with letting waterways surround the forests and letting the tiger return to the mountains—so that the mountains would have their tiger, the forests would have their sparrows, and nature would be able to return to nature. Under a different form of power, however, the tiger would be returned to its cage, and the mountains and waterways would remain under the control of power. Under this latter arrangement, flowers and vegetation may bloom and wilt, but they must endeavor to remain under the control and planning of power so that even the turn of the seasons will remain in the grasp of power.

Contemporary China, however, is not positioned on the side of either power or laxity, but it straddles the two. With centralized power on one side and relative laxity on the other, in contemporary China everything else is positioned in the crotch area between the two. All freedom is performed in this fist-sized crotch area, although this leaves power's legs, waist, and torso completely exhausted and unsettled. Because the uncaged tiger in the crotch area always wants to return to its original territory in the mountains and rivers, you need to feed it in an appropriate and timely fashion. If you feed it too much, you may strengthen it and help it escape, but if you don't feed it enough, it may begin gnawing at the crotch area, leaving a bloody wound. This is China! This is the conflicted relationship between China's centralized power and its unrestrained free market. As for literature, it similarly finds itself caught between the nation's highly centralized political power and its relatively reformed economy.

Centralized power is literature's hazy sky, whereas relative laxity is the sunlight that peeks through that haze. Meanwhile, literature grows, blooms, dances, and breathes under this sky that is alternately overcast and sunny.

THE UNAVOIDABLE RELATIONSHIP BETWEEN WRITING AND POLITICS

Literature can avoid politics the same way that someone who doesn't like fragrant food can be perfectly happy as a vegetarian. Until thirty years ago, China had a policy whereby literature was expected to serve politics, such that literature was part of, and is also positioned beneath, politics. If an author's works didn't attend to politics, then prison would surely attend to the author. Today, however, literature's position has completely changed, and not only does it have the option of not attending to politics, but furthermore—if it has the requisite ability and capacity—it can even supersede and direct politics.

Many authors maintain the position that literature can avoid politics, suggesting that the works of good authors—such as Kafka, who is idolized by Chinese authors—can be discussed independently of politics. The premodern Chinese author Tao Yuanming and the modern author Shen Congwen are respected precisely because they were able to distance themselves from politics and contemporary reality. However, when politics becomes an inextricable part of our daily lives, should we still attempt to avoid it?

Since 1949, politics has continually occupied people's lives. Can intellectuals remove the legacy of the Anti-Rightist Campaign from their lives? During the so-called Three Years of Natural Disaster, more than ten million Chinese starved to death as virtually every family experienced starvation and graves appeared everywhere. Was this the result of centralized political power, or was it simply a natural process caused by locusts and drought? When we consider this disaster, is it possible to describe only the starvation while ignoring the underlying causes, rooted in politics and power?

The Cultural Revolution was a political movement affecting all Chinese, but it was also a decade of daily life.

Today, thirty years later, turbulent politics has by and large receded from our lives (with the notable exception of June Fourth). At the same time, however, politics currently enjoys an even sharper, more fragmented, and more ubiquitous influence over our existence. If we don't attend to how a college student died in a labor camp while playing hide-and-seek or how someone under supervision managed to drown while washing his face, this is because these "unusual events" are viewed as simply random occurrences. However, every incident involving housing, family planning, education, medical treatment, employment, unemployment, internal migration, forced demolition, and urbanization will inevitably be imbricated with elements of corruption, transparency, fairness, justice, the wealth gap, and new class formation. How could these elements ever be completely separated from considerations of politics and power?

The sky above a preschool is full of sunlight and children's innocent fantasies, but if every time you discuss children's education you focus on its corrupt elements, this will inevitably result in making a fuss over nothing. When a novel describes a migrant laborer who comes to the city looking for work, it doesn't necessarily need to focus on the differences between city and countryside, China's employment system and its residency system, or the pressure that urban expansion has been placing on rural areas. We currently find ourselves in a relatively relaxed period that permits the emergence of a variety of different kinds of literature. However, in the same way that even if a preschool is an ideal site for children to grow up, it is also a site of societal education inflected by politics, even if the individual strokes of Chinese characters are completely beautiful and healthy, when considering essays and literary works it is still appropriate and necessary to consider the faults of education. If literature doesn't touch on issues of power and politics, it isn't literature and should be critiqued. In contemporary Chinese society, humanity contains an unprecedented level of complexity, within which every kind of social structure, form, and value can appear. All life, even in the most pristine preschool, is replete with the destructive effects of power and politics. When parents register their children for preschool, accordingly, it would be more useful if, rather than providing the child's name and interests, they could instead specify their own family background, occupation, and position. If parents have a high-ranking and powerful position, this means that their child would inevitably have received more special attention while growing up. Moreover, as soon as children attend preschool, they appreciate the role of power in the secular world. Every year on June 1, Children's Day, there has developed the absurd and perverse tradition whereby parents offer "gifts" to their children's preschool teachers. This practice is common, ordinary, and secular, but at the same time it reflects the alienating effect of politics and power on the secular world. Given the existence of these sorts of customs, can we ever remove power from daily practice? Can we ever excise the corrupting influence of politics and power from even the purest sites, not to mention the encroachment of that corruption into all occupations and departments?

The question we need to consider is "Why is it that literature can distance itself from politics, yet life cannot?" Whereas a family, when dining and conversing, can close its doors and endeavor to keep its daily life separate from social reality, the family is unable to do the same for their children's education, graduation, job assignment, employment, real estate, medical coverage, and countless other basic elements of human existence. When people are unable to distance themselves from these basic elements, they will be unable to liberate their life from the interference and influence of power, politics, and society. Politics and power thoroughly permeate their life and fate. Given that politics has long interfered with Chinese literature (which remains true today), this raises questions about literature's ability to distance itself from the collective consciousness of politics. Literature may be able to distance itself from politics, but what should we do when politics becomes part of our daily existence?

September 11—that terrifying attack that shocked the world—was undoubtedly an appalling international incident. Authors and artists can confront this incident, but we should also permit them to avoid it. If 9/11 eventually becomes a psychological element that permeates the daily life of virtually every American, would literature and art still be able to avoid it and act as though it doesn't exist? That is the question. The influence of Chinese politics on people's lives resembles the psychological impact that 9/11 had on an entire generation. I think it would be incorrect to say that every single American author has focused exclusively on 9/11 and its psychological impact, but it would also be incorrect to say that every American author has assiduously attempted to avoid these topics. We should allow some authors to avoid politics while permitting others to reflect on the reality of politics, power, corruption, and darkness—and this is particularly true of people who live in the shadow of consolidated power. Because one of literature's most important objectives is to describe the complexities of humanity and human emotion, if literature avoids the way in which humanity and human emotion are inextricably intertwined with power, politics, fairness, and freedom, it would be like examining a withered tree while ignoring its environment and seasonal attributes. When politics permeates everyone's daily lives, authors' collective avoidance of politics is ridiculous but also tragic. With respect to contemporary China's complex politics, literature's avoidance of power and politics makes it possible for power and politics to win without even trying.

LITERATURE EXCEEDS POLITICS AND OCCUPIES A GREAT REALM IN WHICH AUTHORS FACE REALITY AND CREATION

In what might appear to be an enlightened and progressive step, politics permits contemporary Chinese authors to use the mantle of "pure literature" to avoid addressing politics directly—like a father who lets his children focus on their studies and not worry about household affairs. However, this practice of permitting authors to *not pay attention* to society, reality, power, and politics while simultaneously *not permitting them* to pay attention to reality, politics, and power is actually a trap. This is a strategy that Chinese politicians have used to intervene in literature and art, and it even takes the form of an anticipatory literary conspiracy. True enlightenment, progress, and reform must allow authors to express their emotions and sentiments toward daily life and thereby attend to the hearts and souls of the people. At the same time, authors must be permitted—and even encouraged—to reflect on how people's existence is oppressed by social reality (including power and politics). They must be permitted to confront reality and attend to people's hearts and the difficulties of human existence. If people's predicament is the result of politics, institutions, and power, then authors must be permitted to examine societal power and political institutions. On the other hand, if the predicament is related to natural resources and environmental factors, authors should be permitted to examine these latter issues. If China's environmental conditions deteriorate to the point that people can't even walk down Beijing's streets without suffocating, shouldn't authors be able to use a literary perspective to reflect on this problem? Everyone knows that China's environmental problems are the result of the nation's unrestrained economic development, which in turn is a result of social and political policies. When authors are attending to environmental concerns and the predicament of human existence, can they also consider social and political policies? Under contemporary writing conditions it is acceptable for literature to focus on environmental concerns if this is done in a strictly "pure" and poetic manner, but if this focus is extended to social and political policy, the result will inevitably be subject to censorship.

Is it true that when art attends to reality, politics, and power, the result is inevitably thoughtful and deep, but when it does not attend to these things, the result is necessarily unthoughtful and shallow? This is a question that all readers and authors must confront, just like the question of whether it is preferable to kill a chicken to get its eggs or to raise the chicken and wait for the eggs to come. Killing the chicken is a kind of end, but it also yields a delicacy, while waiting is a form of anticipation, but it may also be an exercise in futility. Inevitably, every author who wants to answer this question becomes caught in a dilemma between the two alternatives. However, literary creators already have an answer—which is that we cannot ask which are superior, American and British literary works such as Henry David Thoreau's *Walden*, Aldo Leopold's *A Sand County Almanac*, John Haines's *The Stars, the Snow, the Fire: Twenty-Five Years in the Northern Wilderness*, and George Orwell's *1984* and *Animal Farm*, on one hand, or Turkish works such as Orhan Pamuk's *Snow*, on the other. Just as we can't say definitively which is better, seafood or meat, monkey head mushroom or swallow's nest soup, Peking Opera or my hometown's Henan Opera, American country music or jazz, when it comes to questions of value, literary works can't really be compared with one another.

When writing distances itself from politics and power, it becomes a kind of creative output. However, even when it approaches politics and power, it is still a kind of creative output. Given that for the past century—and particularly since 1949—Chinese authors have continually found their art to be oppressed by the forces of revolution, politics, and power, so artists, readers, and critics have reached an understanding whereby literature that distances itself from politics is regarded as a kind of "pure art," whereas literature that approaches reality and politics is deemed to be "serious." The former permits, and even encourages, literature to avoid contemporary reality. Like popular genre fiction (such as time-travel literature and ghost stories), beautiful writing about self, emotions, and youth that is popular among a younger generation of authors can be praised, although in these works one is not permitted to reflect on contemporary reality and people's predicaments. Authors who are willing to shoulder the responsibility of examining history and contemporary reality are given a more specific assignment, in that when they are attending to contemporary reality—which is to say, life permeated by power and politics—they are expected to stand on a higher level such that their literature not only attends to contemporary reality but also *exceeds* that same reality. When attending to politics, not only are authors expected to focus on politics, nonpolitical life, and life politics, but they must also exceed the life politics and the life permeated by politics.

For authors, this kind of literature should exceed lived politics and political life, and particularly social life that is completely permeated by politics—which is different from the oft-cited principle that literature must transcend politics. The basic meaning of the verb *transcend* means to exceed something, the same way that for a race car to overtake another, the two vehicles must be on the same track. In discussions of Chinese literature, however, this process of transcending refers instead to the process of avoiding politics and reality. This kind of writing that departs from the racetrack—meaning that it distances itself from social life and avoids the factors that are the most direct cause of people's predicament—is described as transcending reality, but it may also be called a form of soft writing. By extension, writing that confronts reality head-on may be called a form of hard writing.

Indeed, Chinese literature is either a direct form of hard writing or else a distanced form of soft writing. However, when it comes to hard writing that does not attempt to avoid contradictions, and specifically does not attempt to avoid real life that is permeated by politics, what is most taboo is the type of superficial and simple approach that cannot exceed reality. Meanwhile, the process of exceeding reality expects that hard writing will never abandon its attempt to grasp people's predicaments, their emotion and soul, and their spiritual situation within social reality.

China's Chongqing Incident attracted worldwide attention, and everyone understands that it was a function of Chinese politics. Although Chinese people constantly discuss this topic at the dinner table and in teahouses, no Chinese author has yet expressed any interest in writing about it. Why is this? On one hand, it is because the incident is simply too political and too sensitive, but on the other hand it is also because many Chinese authors feel that this topic is simply too real, to the point that it would be difficult for a literary representation to surpass the political implications of the incident itself. By extension, if we consider the claim that the realm in which authors face reality is one in which literature exceeds politics, then this principle demands that if authors have the requisite ability and experience with the Chongqing Incident, then when they write about it, they will see through the political mist and focus on the incident's protagonists Bo Xilai and Gu Kailai and their son Bo Guagua, together with Wang Tiejun, the British businessman Neil Haywood, and an assortment of other figures, as well as the spiritual predicament of the residents of Chongqing themselves. Authors must understand that when it comes to the existential and spiritual predicament of these sorts of powerful and high-positioned figures, their inner heart and soul are inherently more anxious, more vain, and more complex than those of ordinary people like ourselves.

If a literary work could begin from this sort of higher and greater level and write about everyone involved in the Chongqing Incident by focusing on their souls and their predicament, then this might count as the author occupying what we might call a "higher and greater realm." To put this point more simply, Truman Capote's *In Cold Blood* attempted to exceed the incident that inspired the novel (although it also must be admitted that the tragic murder in 1960s America that is described in the novel was unrelated to politics), and we cannot but concede that it succeeded in penetrating the incident and returning to humanity's soul, and in this way it transcended the incident itself. Similarly, Gabriel García Márquez's *The Fall of the Patriarch* also exceeded politics and was able to return to literature itself. Of course, the greatest example of this phenomenon is China's own *Dream of the Red Chamber*. Why did Mao Zedong characterize this work as a thoroughly political "history of the decline of feudal bourgeoisie"? This is because in this great novel, the site of Grand Prospect Garden is permeated by politics and power. If we could excavate all the novel's soil, we would find the white bones and decayed flesh of politics and power. However, because of Cao Xueqin's greatness, he allowed his work to exceed what we call reality, society, power, and politics, and returned it to a realm of people interacting with people. As a result, the work is no longer a novel of lived politics or political life, and instead it is an immortal literary masterpiece.

To return to the Chongqing Incident, if Capote had written about this incident, the result would have been a novel documenting everyone's inner heart. If García Márquez had written about it, the result would have been a new magical realist chronicle of a fictional and imaginary clan. And if Cao Xueqin had written about it, the result would have been a masterpiece that truly exceeds this political incident itself. As a Chinese reader and author, when I speak of the possibility of this incident exceeding reality, what I hope is that the Chongqing Incident could become a new *Dream of the Red Chamber*.

WHAT I GAIN AND LOSE BY WRITING AT THE LEVEL OF POWER AND POLITICS

Let me return to the topic of my own writing.

To tell the truth, I don't think my works are particularly remarkable. China has many outstanding authors, whose works surge forth as irrepressibly as the nation's economy—but these works are also accompanied by toadyism, weakness, absurdity, and distortion. These works' toadyism and weakness are the authors' tragedy, and although social reality's absurdity and distortion are bad for society and the nation, they can nevertheless be good for literature. As long as authors dare to confront power and reality, to write in the midst of absurdity, and to reflect in the midst of distortion, the tree of literature will continue to produce countless different branches, leaves, and fruits. This is like a sapling that sprouts out of a fissure in a cliff wall, grows in a distorted manner, but ultimately becomes a thing of beauty.

This is Chinese literature. All authors live in an absurd, cruel, and diverse reality in which they write all sorts of works, cultivate all sorts of readers, and challenge all sorts of critics. When I refer to the act of "writing under centralized power and relative laxity," I am referring to a literature that is distorted and deformed, and that is characterized by contradiction and reflection. For an author writing in a Chinese climate that is half water and half fire, half-stormy and half-clear, sometimes cold and sometimes warm, sometimes dry and sometimes icy, this is literature's existence and its resistance.

Under these "sometimes cold and sometimes warm" conditions, soft writing receives warmth but hard writing receives coldness. In the short term, however, neither will be able to cross over and compromise, although both will be enterprising and will put their ability to good use. Therefore, they will have no choice but to pause at this juncture, summarize the present, and consider the future—so that in their subsequent efforts to exceed reality they won't break their pen while attempting to write.

In my own writing, meanwhile, I have never abandoned my efforts to examine China's history and contemporary reality. This kind of focus can make you feel extremely anxious and can leave you unable to view people— or at least Chinese people—with an acceptable and enjoyable degree of beauty. As a result, this approach makes virtually all readers assume that this kind of hard writing contains a form of resistance. I wouldn't deny this claim, although I do want to specify that if everyone views things in such a simple manner, then the "soft and beautiful" and the "warm and loving" side of one's works will ultimately be obscured. Over time, one's works—located in this intermediary realm between praise and critique—will become hesitant and lose their identity, their center, and their ability to express the author's sensibility toward beauty and sadness.

Perhaps it is true that I am losing this sensibility. Because my writing is too focused on how people are oppressed by society, power, and contemporary reality, it risks losing its ability to appreciate individuals as such. I must therefore remain vigilant about this possibility and attempt to compensate for it. Within my own hard writing, I must endeavor to draw on soft writing's tenderness and beauty.

It cannot be denied that Chinese authors live and write in this distorted environment of centralized power and relative laxity, but one must remain vigilant about writing that deliberately distances itself from China's acute contradictions and from a certain historical and contemporary life that is permeated by politics. In the area of relative laxity where sunlight peeks through, there are grass and flowers, beauty and tenderness, as well as an attitude of contentment with respect to the dilemma of survival. Hard writing cannot reject a more literary soft writing, and in its attempt to exceed reality, hard writing must continue to draw nourishment from soft writing. Only then may it surpass Capote's *In Cold Blood* and twentieth-century literature's barrier of absurdity and magic, and produce a new, modern Chinese-style *Dream of the Red Chamber*.

Second, this focus on reality and the idolization of hard writing has made me lose my attention to, care for, and love of ordinary people's daily lives. My attachment to the land has also become murky because of the dullness of everyday life. The focus of my writing should not depart from the land where I was born and raised, just as Faulkner's focus could not depart from his fictional Yoknapatawpha County. It has been thirty years since I left my hometown, and although I return every year, I increasingly feel that I have little to say to the people who live there, for we no longer share a common language or way of thinking. Now when I return, it is as though I go there not because I am originally from there but rather because I am simply visiting relatives. I no longer understand the villagers' jokes, arguments, and gossip or the strong emotions aroused by their attempts to secure daily provisions, much less their intense pursuit of material life and the calm manner with which they approach spiritual barrenness. Perhaps it is true that I no longer belong there and that I only return because I need to collect stories, characters, and plotlines for my novels.

Every time I return home, I sit for a long time with my elder brother without saying a word.

Every time I return home, I sleep in the same room as my mother, but I no longer want to hear her retell the same old stories about fellow villagers' aging, illnesses, and death.

It seems that I rarely sit with my elder sisters to discuss my nieces' and nephews' lives and careers.

This is true, and it is also terrifying. It reflects the boredom I have come to feel about that land, my loss of emotion, and how I have lost patience for daily life. Moreover, every day I feel more disgust for worldly affairs and feel more numb toward human emotion.

Third, because of my attempt to exceed reality, my writings have lost their sensitivity and love for the small. If hard and soft writing are established in my works, then my large and small writing (and here, these terms refer not to the length of a work, but rather to whether the work reflects on large or small concerns) can also be established. For instance, based on its breadth, length, and depth, Tolstoy's fiction can be characterized as large writing, whereas Chekhov's can be characterized as relatively small. But how can one say that because Chekhov writes about small characters and minor incidents, his writing itself is inferior to Tolstoy's? Actually, their small and large writings are equally great, and both were blessed with immortal literary value. Furthermore, much of the time Chekhov's small approach can do without Tolstoy's large one, although Tolstoy's large approach cannot do without Chekhov's small one—the same way that Anna Karenina cannot *not* have servants at her side, although a minor civil servant would be perfectly happy not to have a general by his side. *War and Peace* is about so many generals and officers, but without the thousands of ordinary soldiers, how could there be war and peace?

Because of my attention to the power, politics, society, and reality in the sky over people's heads, I risk losing my appreciation of ordinary people, emotion, and affairs. I risk losing my sensitivity to the small in literature. In my writings about power and politics, I emphasize the large over the small, the hard over the soft. Perhaps my writing is currently heading toward a deviation and derailment. Under a sky of centralized power and relative laxity, I can't focus only on the haze of centralized power, and instead I must smile as I consider that ray of sunlight of laxity that peeks through the haze.

In the end, the sky will clear up and people will smile again. As we write under the haze of centralized power, we should endeavor to let the future light shine out of the tip of our pen.

10 Living without Dignity but Writing with Honor

Looking at nineteenth-century Russian literature is like backing into a dense forest of birch trees, in that the scenery does not part in front of us but rather gradually slides open as we pass. On one side there is Tolstoy, and on the other side there is Dostoevsky, and what distinguishes them is not merely their works themselves but also their respective lives and environment. Tolstoy enjoyed an aristocratic or near-aristocratic life, whereas Dostoevsky came from a plebeian or even impoverished background; consequently, their lives and spirit—together with their corresponding view of literature and of the world—diverged dramatically. In Tolstoy's works one finds a luxurious, dignified, and open atmosphere, whereas in Dostoevsky's one finds a poor, broken, and entangled pattern. However, Tolstoy's works are not necessarily more noble than Dostoevsky's; in fact, the dignity contained in their writings is virtually indistinguishable.

From this, we can offer the following observations:

1 An author's life and heart may help determine the relative brightness or darkness of his or her works.

2 The nobility of a work is intimately related to the nobility of the author's life.

3 If an author lives a life lacking in dignity, however, this does not necessarily mean that his or her works will be similarly lacking in honor.

What I wish to discuss below, accordingly, is the phenomenon of living without dignity but writing with honor.

LIVING WITHOUT DIGNITY

Throughout China's history, everything that one class of people did — from the clothes they wore to where they walked, what they ate and drank, and even what they used to wipe their mouth after they spit — inevitably revealed their noble status. Like the characters in Tolstoy's novels, this class of people was mostly cut from the same cloth. But for another class of people, major issues like their home, work, career, marriage, and even their birth and death are handled in a very casual fashion, without a trace of dignity — like Dostoevsky's tormented characters, Chekhov's public servants, or Balzac's money-obsessed Parisians. People living without dignity must constantly struggle to maintain the honor they need to survive — this is everyone's most basic need. When added together, these basic desires coalesce into a human ideal.

For instance, in *The Hunchback of Notre-Dame*, Quasimodo leads a miserable existence but earns everyone's respect, which is why readers around the world are moved by his story. In human society, people may be either elite or debased, and nineteenth-century literature seems to address these issues in a broader and richer manner than does twentieth-century literature. In contrast to nineteenth-century literature, twentieth-century literature is more interested in individuals and their lives. This is because twentieth-century works place considerable emphasis on the dignity with which people live their lives, but it is also because these same works begin to address these issues in a more abstract and philosophical manner, and consequently pull away from the experiences of readers' daily lives. Examples of the latter include the character Josef K in Kafka's fiction and the figure of the stranger in Camus's novel, together with assorted characters in works by authors who placed even greater emphasis on fictional form. Eventually, there emerged conceptual literature, in which authors wrote about abstract concepts and ideals. In the mid- to late 1980s, Chinese literature underwent a significant realization with respect to individual existence. This was possible because Chinese authors realized that people's spiritual lives are grounded on a foundation determined by their specific material conditions. In the past, the saying *When one's belly is full, one's thoughts turn to debauchery* was often used to describe Chinese people's lives, suggesting that after people have eaten their fill, they then turn their attention to romance and sex rather than to philosophical questions such as "Where did we come from, and where are we going?" Chinese people and intellectuals do not place as much emphasis on the individual or on spiritual concerns, and instead they focus on material matters such as money, food, and sex. This is why for millennia Chinese people's lives have been shaped by material factors rather than by issues of spiritual dignity.

Living without dignity—this is a stark reality for many Chinese people. As a result, most of our literary works depict people's abject lives, not how they might live with dignity. This is simply how life is, and it is also what is represented in fiction. Chinese-style realism always contends that literary representation should be derived from—yet be better than—real life. On this point, good authors adopt the slogan "Make a concerted effort" and use it as both a collective platitude and a means of resistance. As result, Chinese realism has not surpassed real life but remains suspended on the surface of reality. Virtually everyone in contemporary China lives abjectly and without dignity—including the rich and the poor, officials and ordinary people. When struggling to secure basic provisions such as oil, salt, and vinegar, ordinary people and the poor have no opportunity to consider issues of human rights. So-called human rights are something people can enjoy only once they have enough to eat.

Meanwhile, people who have become rich in contemporary China's industrial age are able to drive fancy cars, live in expensive mansions, and employ personal secretaries (and often have inappropriate relationships with their secretaries and chauffeurs). They enjoy enormous influence and respect but must still bow unctuously whenever they encounter a section chief, division chief, or bureau chief. Why is this? It is because they used power to obtain their wealth and position. In contemporary Chinese society, if people from business and industry don't link up with power, they have no hope of obtaining profit or capital. In contemporary China, dignity is guaranteed not by the law but rather by power. To live a life of dignity, accordingly, one must live a life of power.

Why has the worship and critique of power become such a popular topic among Chinese authors—including young and old, men and women, famous and unknown? There is almost no other country in the world where authors are as obsessed with understanding and describing power as they are in China. It is a peculiar characteristic of contemporary China that there is no author who has not written about power. Is it because of love and hate that we find this intimate and widespread description of power in contemporary literature? In fact, it is precisely because power has become, for contemporary Chinese, the ultimate guarantee and destroyer of dignity. This also applies to those people who already possess power. China's most honest joke is "If you haven't been to Beijing, you won't know what it means to be a small bureaucrat, and if you haven't been to Shenzhen, you won't know what it means to have little money." I once met a town mayor who went to the county seat, and when he returned, he exclaimed, "Fuck, I don't even live as well as the common people there. The county head cursed me the way he would curse his grandson!" I also once met a county-level cadre who went to Beijing on business, then waited outside the residence of a higher cadre to whom he wanted to offer a gift. He began unctuously speaking to the guard, trying to determine whether the higher cadre was home or when he would return—as a peasant might do when trying to see a county-level cadre. After the guard reprimanded him, the county-level cadre returned to his hotel, took the gift he had brought, and hurled it to the ground, exclaiming, "Fuck, I'm not even as good as a peasant!" But how could he have known that when peasants try to see a village head or township chief, they are humiliated in a similar manner? Of course, this does not mean that those high-ranking cadres enjoy more dignity in the face of power. Power is an endless chain, and when high cadres meet a national official, when a national official meets the US president, or when the US president encounters the people who control his votes and his reputation, they experience a blow to their dignity. Only in a country like China is power positioned above all else. In this country's putrid system, when power is the fundamental guarantee of people's dignity, it becomes the ultimate trap.

In short, the inevitable conclusion is that no one in contemporary society can live with dignity. Not only is it exceedingly common for people in contemporary China to live a life without dignity; the vast majority are trapped in this position, and this is a reality they have no choice but to confront. This brings us to our next issue.

When someone doesn't even have the right to be a person but nevertheless wants to secure a modicum of dignity, he or she must recognize society's customs and voluntarily follow a secular life. For many authors and intellectuals in contemporary China, recognizing society's customs is a conscious and necessary choice that they must make. First, these authors and intellectuals come to view the world itself as secular, whereas the peasants who make up 90 percent of China's population must live an unbearably vulgar existence in which they know little, are short-sighted and selfish, and are full of absurd desires.

Lu Xun once remarked that laughable people have detestable qualities. Who was he referring to? He was referring to the country's peasants and all the people living in Chinese society at that time. Among contemporary Chinese authors, no one was more penetrating than Lu Xun—yet even Lu Xun was utterly lacking in sympathy and understanding when it came to ordinary people, and particularly those who had received little or no education. He felt that they were uncultured, secular, and unbearably vulgar. This understanding became a traditional belief that intellectuals passed down from one generation to the next, based on the understanding that peasants are inherently vulgar and depraved.

With respect to merchants and powerful officials in traditional China, meanwhile, our ancestors studied for the imperial exams to become government officials and enjoy a golden life of money and power, even as those same officials looked down on the common people. Our ancestors viewed merchants and officials as vulgar and secular, while at the same time striving to become like them.

After workers, peasants, and merchants became secularized, the only remaining group was made up of those with "learning"—which is to say, the literati. Given that the world has become secularized, literati should also embrace the secular life. I know a famous Chinese professor who is very eloquent, and whenever he lectures, virtually all his female students inevitably become infatuated with him. Once he steps off the podium, however, all the female students fear him—because he likes young women. This professor travels around the country, and whenever he arrives at a new location, he gives lectures during the day, and then each night he visits foot-washing and massage parlors to look for young women. While he is enjoying himself with these young women, he simultaneously encourages them to study hard and remake themselves—to become pure and meaningful people. Of course, after parting, he calls the women sluts and complains that they are the most debased people in the world. Countless Chinese intellectuals are like this absurdly self-conflicted professor, and in daily life they are hedonists, sectarians, and the most stereotypical intellectuals and secular figures.

Given that even contemporary intellectuals are like this, what can we possibly expect of China's workers, peasants, and soldiers?

This brings us back to the issue of writing. Given that authors belong to the category of intellectuals, it is perhaps to be expected that they would identify as secularists. Like poets, painters, and artists, the dissolute attitude with which authors view women is something they may regard as an imperial right. After all, if they were not dissolute, what kind of poet or artist would they be? Similarly, when authors identify with a secular life, they also regard this as an imperial right. This is because in Chinese literature, fiction has always been the product of open-air performance venues, just as stories are told by the common people. It is believed that literature originates from day-to-day life, and given that fiction is a product of open-air performance venues, how can its creators not be intimately familiar with day-to-day life? How can they not recognize and participate in secular life? How can they themselves not become secular?

A couple of years ago, there was a literary scandal when many of China's contemporary authors collectively copied the text of Mao Zedong's "Talks at the Yan'an Forum." This incident was closely followed by people around the world who pay attention to Chinese literature and culture, and it received renewed attention after Mo Yan was awarded the Nobel Prize. I see this incident as being a result of contemporary authors, after having already identified with and participated in secular life, feeling that they might as well do so again. We could compare this to the way peasants view all grain as valuable and scarce, to the point that they don't hesitate to pick up kernels from the ground or even from filthy piles of dung. We should certainly respect those authors who refused to copy Mao's "Talks," but we must also try to understand the motivation of those who did agree to do so. Actually, the latter agreed because they were living a secular and entirely undignified life! They wanted to derive dignity not from personal character but rather from power. When Chinese authors seek respect, they must recognize a secular life—and to recognize a secular life, they must recognize and approach power. In the end, they must claim the honor associated with power. This is a choice that Chinese authors must make.

Let me speak about myself.

I didn't help copy Mao's "Talks," but this doesn't necessarily mean that I have more integrity or am more enlightened than others, and it certainly doesn't mean that I don't recognize a secular life. It's not that everyone else is dirt and weeds while I am a fresh flower or medicinal herb, or a valuable bamboo of virtue in a Zheng Banqiao painting. That's not it at all! I am also a product of the secular world, and in many respects I am very secular. For instance, when I was young, I joined the army, and after I reached the position of department or section head, whenever I returned home I would always have to take some cigarettes and liquor to the house of our village head and sit for a while. In the Chinese administrative system, the village head has a ranking equivalent to that of a squad leader in the military. Many squad leaders subsequently returned to their villages and became village heads and Party branch secretaries. But sometimes the village head wields more power than a regiment or division commander and is responsible for overseeing a community of several hundred—or even several thousand—people. Given that my own parents, brother, sister-in-law, and other siblings were all overseen by this village head, did I have any choice but to offer him cigarettes and liquor? What kind of behavior is this? This is what we call recognizing secular realities. If one wants to live with dignity, one must begin by living without dignity. I'm currently in my fifties, and our village head is still a young man, yet every time I return home he always says, "Have Yan Lianke come over to my place to sit for a while," whereupon I have no choice but to go over to his place and "sit for a while."

This is a small matter, but next I will discuss something more significant. I am an author and have already entered the second half century of my life. Someone once asked me whether I would accept a position as county head, bureau chief, or department chief if it were to be offered to me. I replied that no, I probably wouldn't. Then the other person asked, if I'm not willing to bow my head to power and accept the guilt of being an official, then what if I were offered a position as director of the Chinese Bureau of Culture or the Propaganda Bureau—certainly, I wouldn't be able to resist the appeal of this sort of power? I replied that it would be hypocritical to say that I could resist this sort of offer, for this would imply that I might be made the offer in the first place. The other person said, if you can't resist this sort of offer, then you need to continue bowing to power, and in that trap of linking dignity to power you must rescue yourself and others, and protect yourself and others. Actually, I'm not like the great poet Qu Yuan, and I know very well in what respects I am vulgar. At most, all I can claim is that, on account of my age, experience, and fate, I have attained some understanding of the secular world. But, in the end, I am still a secular individual and someone who accepts the secular world.

This brings us to our next issue.

BEING A PERSON IN A SECULAR WORLD, BUT STRIVING TO AVOID BEING A SECULAR PERSON

At the end of the day, we are all human and aspire to live with dignity. In the reality of contemporary China, where everything is restricted and trapped by power, if we wish to be human in a secular world, we must make every effort to become a secular person, and even if we can't completely accomplish this, we must at least attempt to partially do so. I have a cousin, and one of his experiences offered a compelling mirror of my own life. As the number and age of the children in a rural household increase, so does the pressure on the members of the next generation to split off from extended family and set up their own households. To split off from the family, however, members of the next generation need a homestead of their own, but in China individuals are not allowed to own land. All land belongs to the state, and if you want to build a house or work the land, you must first petition state and government representatives for permission.

"Peasants are the owners of the land." In China, this claim is a farce—false and meaningless. My cousin heroically resisted the state's family-planning policy and had numerous children. He had so many children that they couldn't all live in his home, and therefore they wanted to be assigned a homestead to build a new house. To do this, he would have needed to give his village head countless gifts, but he adamantly refused to send any gifts, to the point that he preferred not to have a homestead at all. This was not done in a fit of pique but rather was a result of stubbornness. My cousin didn't believe that the world or people's feelings could ever become so dark. He resisted for more than ten years, as he and his family of five or six continued to live in the same one-room dwelling. When his children grew up, they couldn't get married, and it wasn't until the entire village felt that it was unacceptable that this cousin still did not have a homestead that the village committee finally assigned him a piece of land with poor feng shui and poor access. As a result, my cousin was convinced that the world was not so corrupt that there was absolutely no way out, saying to himself: "Isn't it true that they eventually granted me some land for a new house?"

This is an excellent example of Ah Q's strategy of seeking a spiritual victory. But this cousin increasingly made me feel that he deserved my respect. I felt that his actions reflected not so much a sense of stubbornness but rather a deep sense of dignity. I frequently look to him as a model. He recognizes secular customs while also working to understand and embrace those customs and the people of the world.

Gandhi was right when he said that "no one in this world is my enemy." Even Liu Xiaobo, who is currently imprisoned, similarly insists that "no one in this world is my enemy." This is a belief that only great people can have. In their struggle for freedom, however, who is their opponent, adversary, and enemy? It is racial and class power! From this perspective, to be an author—to be perpetually examining people's spirit—means that one must fully understand secular customs and love all people. It is possible for us not to have belief, but we cannot lack credibility as individuals; it is possible not to find the truth, but we cannot abandon our determination to continue looking; we can never resist everything in every possible context, but it is possible to refuse to do certain specific things in this disgusting, secular world.

If one cannot speak, one can always remain silent. I prefer to stand silently by the side of the road rather than walk down the middle of the road surrounded by applause and fresh flowers. It is possible that one may fail to achieve one's goals, but one cannot stop struggling on their behalf. It is only in this way that we can come to have dignity. Otherwise, we would truly sink to the level of Ah Q and Old Chuan in Lu Xun's stories, the civil servants in Chekhov's and Balzac's works, or Josef K in Kafka's *The Trial*.

Even if it is impossible to resist everything, one must still struggle not to simply ingratiate oneself with power. This is a very low standard, but if all of China's intellectuals adopted this attitude, I think it would be possible for them to maintain a modicum of dignity.

WRITING WITH DIGNITY

The question of how to write with dignity is a vast topic that I can address here only in a brief and cursory manner. Among China's authors and intellectuals, it is one thing to live with dignity and another thing altogether to write with dignity. From their biographies, we can see that Tolstoy's life was more serious and dignified than Dostoevsky's, but their works are similarly serious and dignified. In fact, if we focus on their works and fictional characters, I feel that Dostoevsky's are somewhat more dignified than Tolstoy's. From Kafka's biography, we see that he led an ordinary and even vulgar life, but the dignity with which he treats humanity in his works is something no other author can match. Similarly, Somerset Maugham led a very vulgar life and could frequently be found laughing and chatting in the street, but the dignity one finds in his works is undeniable. The best example of this phenomenon is Alexandre Dumas père and fils. Who was the better writer? There is, of course, no question. If we were to put *The Count of Monte Cristo*, *The Three Musketeers*, and *Camille* side by side, we would have to acknowledge that *Camille* is far more dignified than the other two. Applied to Chinese writers, this suggests that even if one must live without dignity, it is still possible to write with solemnity. That is to say, even if a writer's life is vulgar for reasons beyond his or her control, he or she nevertheless can—and must—achieve dignity through his or her writing. To achieve dignity through one's writing is the foundation of what it means to be an author in the first place. When an author's writing loses this sense of independence and dignity, their writings cease to be literature and instead writing becomes just a job—a task that one performs simply to be able to buy food and clothing, and to survive.

In short, it is possible to lead a vulgar life, but one must still strive to write with dignity.

To write with dignity has several implications. First, one must respect literature itself. In their daily life, Chinese writers sometimes have no choice but to separate literature from real life. In their daily life, they may be unable to free themselves from vulgarity, although in their writing they can do so and, in the process, attain a certain level of dignity. Mario Vargas Llosa was once almost elected president of Peru, but I can't understand his fascination with power and politics. If you want to talk about vulgarity, I feel that this represents the pinnacle of vulgarity. However, this experience did not influence his faith in and devotion to literature or his understanding and writing of literature. Would you say that Václav Havel was just an author or a politician? As a politician, he changed the direction and fate of his nation. As an author, his participation in politics is without equal. But if we read China's "internal" edition of Havel's *Collected Works*, we also see that as an author, Havel's dignity—and here we will speak only of his dignity—was truly awe inspiring and makes us feel inferior by comparison.

Second, one must maintain a dignified understanding of the secular world. Even as one inhabits the secular world, one must strive to write with dignity and not simply write in a secular fashion. On this point, Chekhov is a model. Each of his fictional characters lives a completely secular life, but he nevertheless manages to compose each of them with dignity. Similarly, most of the characters in Guy de Maupassant's story "Butterball" appear to possess a great sense of dignity, and only the prostitute Elisabeth Rousset, also known as Butterball, appears vulgar. But de Maupassant, in this tableau, manages to draw out the dignity of his most secular character. Twentieth-century literature has a more self-aware and fundamental understanding of people, and consequently its sense of dignity is more obvious.

Third, there is the issue of how Chinese authors can write with dignity. To write with dignity involves a kind of attitude, a kind of position, and a kind of conscious choice. Someone whose life is not very serious and solemn can nevertheless write dignified works. Conversely, however, someone who lives a dignified life will not necessarily write dignified works. That is to say, the dignity of a literary work is not necessarily determined by the kind of life that the author leads. Instead, a work's dignity is determined by the author's literary perspective and understanding of literature, not by his or her views on life. However, we should also probably acknowledge that it is easier for someone who lives with dignity to write dignified works. Lu Xun's life was very solemn and dignified, and all his works are similarly very dignified. However, the poet Guo Moruo represents a different kind of model, in that his early poetry and drama are without a doubt quite dignified, although this is less true of his later works, which are not only rather kitschy but also quite vulgar. Why is this? This was dictated by Guo Moruo's life and his views on life and the world. When Guo Moruo lost his sense of dignity and began worshipping power, he found himself unable to continue writing dignified works and unable to enter a process of dignified production. That is to say, dignified writing does not necessarily derive from an author's dignified life, but in order to write dignified works throughout one's entire life, one must maintain a consistently dignified attitude toward both life and literature.

China is a nation of slogans, and I hope you will permit me to conclude here with some anti-slogan slogans:

Recognize secular life, but be a dignified person in a secular world.

Live in the secular world, but don't enter into secular writing.

Don't demand that others write with dignity, but strive for dignity in your own writing.

11 My Ideal Is Simply to Write a Novel That I Think Is Good

The relationship between literature and ideals is a familiar yet beautiful topic.

Below, I will unpack this topic by identifying several keywords and then pursue a process of disassembly and explanation.

FIRST, MY IDEALS . . .

To address my ideals, let me consider a few incidents from my childhood.

One incident occurred when I was still as small as a baby rabbit emerging from its burrow for the first time to sun itself, or a lamb leaving its pen for the first time to look for a tasty clump of grass. At the time I was seven or eight, and my hunger was like a chain around my neck that left me hanging in midair, constricting my throat until it resembled a dead branch or blade of grass through which no air could pass. Like a discus thrower, I would hurl my life into an overgrown grave. It was at that point that my father sent me a message inviting me to visit him at his construction site twenty *li* away because he had some meat to share. So early one morning I set off to go see him, and on my way I repeatedly stopped to ask for directions, afraid that I wouldn't be able to find him. I arrived at the construction site at around noon, and when my father saw me, he patted my head and took me to the site's cook, who in turn led me into a small room and handed me a bowl of boiled pork—because it turns out that the construction site had just slaughtered a pig. The cook also gave me a steamed bun, then closed the paper-covered window and locked the door so that no one would see me.

In that pitch-black room I gobbled down the food as quickly as possible. In no time I not only finished all the pork but also drank a bowl of greasy broth. That was when I realized that white pork is more fragrant than red pork and that fatty pork is tastier than lean pork. As I emerged from the room holding my belly and was preparing to leave, my father asked, "Did you eat it all? You didn't save any for your elder sister?" During that period my sister was often ill and bedridden. I gazed into my father's eyes and immediately regretted having been so greedy—like someone who picks up something on the side of the road and is then accused of being a thief. That afternoon, I took a piece of pork my father couldn't bring himself to eat and wrapped it in paper to take home. I walked home without saying a word, lacking the joy I had felt while actually eating the pork. When I now think back to that day, I still feel guilty and humiliated.

The second incident involved a fellow villager who had a scalp disease that had made him lose his hair. He was a young man, and everyone called him Baldy. He wore hats all year around—padded hats in winter, single-layer hats in summer, and straw hats when it was especially hot. Because this young man was bald and his scalp was disfigured, almost no one ever tried to remove his hat—and if someone did, the man would curse and fight as though his life depended on it, and might even try to bash the other person's head with a brick. This is because for the young man his hat was not merely a hat; it also represented his sacred dignity.

One day when the villagers were eating in the entranceway, the director of the township Party committee—at that time it was called a revolutionary committee—suddenly grabbed the young man's hat and tossed it into the air, where it spun around before falling to the ground. The young man cried out and tried to smash the man's head with his rice bowl. At the last minute, however, he suddenly realized that the person who had thrown his hat was actually the revolutionary committee director, which was a position equivalent to a township head or Party secretary.

For several seconds, it was so quiet you could hear a pen drop. The young man slowly lowered his rice bowl and looked apologetically at the revolutionary committee director. Then he silently walked past the director, silently picked up his hat, and silently placed it back on his head. Finally, still holding his rice bowl, the young man silently returned home.

As the young man walked away, he appeared weak and listless, like an autumn leaf fluttering to the ground. In my mind, this leaf has drifted all the way from my youth to my middle age. It still hasn't found a place to land, and instead continues to drift through my memory.

The third incident involves the construction site I just mentioned, where a construction team was building a bridge over the river in front of our village. Dating back to the very beginning of creation, when the deity Pangu first separated Heaven and Earth, that was our village's very first cement bridge made from reinforced concrete. The leading bridge-construction company in Zhengzhou, the provincial capital, came to build the bridge, and the workers included a married couple from Guangdong who stayed in our home. The couple liked to eat dog meat, which was somewhat off-putting, but they also had a daughter a year younger than I. Her name was Jianna, and she was quite pretty, she dressed well, and when she walked, her footsteps sounded like someone playing the piano. She called me "Brother Lianke" and always held my hand on our way to and from school. I would carry her book bag for her and thought that life was so filled with bright sunlight, spring warmth, and fragrant flowers that even the rain and sleet sounded like a pair of youths running through the fields. However, before one vacation period I went to stay for a few days with my aunt in the mountains, and when I returned home, I found that the new bridge now towered over the river in front of the village. The couple who came to build the bridge and the girl who always held my hand and called me Brother Lianke—they had all left with the construction company and relocated elsewhere.

Jianna left me her aluminum pencil case as a memento and disappeared, and I never saw her again except in my memory. Even after I wrote her into my novels to serve as a missing-person notice, I never saw her again.

My melancholy was like a bygone rainy season, and the bygone era was like the rainy season's melancholy. Along the way I went from being a child to a youth, and when I was twenty, I left home to join the army. My first dinner at the recruitment company consisted of meat buns. That day, I consumed eighteen meat buns, each of which was as large as a steamed bun (another recruit from my hometown ate twenty-two). The next day we had dumplings, and each of the soldiers in my company ate an average of more than a *jin* of dumplings. I heard the recruit company commander on the phone with the battalion commander, reporting on the state of these new recruits and complaining, "These poor boys eat like pigs!" Even as he cursed us, we—or at least I—did not get angry. I didn't respond like that young man from our village with the scalp disease, who was furious with the revolutionary committee director.

In that military camp in eastern Henan I rode a train for the first time and also watched television for the first time. I watched volleyball on television and learned that China's women's volleyball team had won three world championships. Even more importantly, I read my first foreign novel, which was Margaret Mitchell's *Gone with the Wind*. It was only then that I realized that in China one could also read foreign novels in translation. Up to that point, all I had read were China's "Red Classics." I thought all fiction from around the world was just like China's—where, if 70 or 80 percent of a story is about revolution and 20 or 30 percent is about love, then you'll have 100 percent of a good novel. It was *Gone with the Wind* that made me realize that there were countless other works that were not only better than China's revolutionary stories; they were also completely different. The reason these other works were better is precisely because they were so different. I used *Gone with the Wind* as a bridge to world literature and went on to read works by Balzac, Tolstoy, Dostoevsky, Hugo, Stendhal, Flaubert, Chekhov, O. Henry, Jack London, and others. I read all the great eighteenth- and nineteenth-century works I could find, and after I finished them I began writing in my spare time. As I searched my memory, the significance of these three childhood incidents underwent a transformation because of my subsequent experience with reading literature.

I originally thought I had run twenty *li* to eat a bowl of fatty pork because I was hungry, but subsequently my experience with reading literature helped me understand that I had done so not merely because of hunger but also because of ideals. I ran to the construction site because I held on to an ideal that, in the future, I would be able to eat enough and eat well.

Originally, I believed that the reason why the young man in my village with the scalp disease did not fight the director of the revolutionary committee was because he feared compromise, but later reading literature made me realize that he also felt the respect and terror that virtually everyone feels toward power.

Originally, I believed that my separation from Jianna was the result of a completely innocent, first-love melancholy, but later reading literature helped me understand that it was a result of my yearning and pursuit of a certain kind of urban civilization.

This was my childhood yearning and pursuit: I yearned to eat well, I yearned for people's respect, and I yearned for modern urban civilization. When these three yearnings were combined, they formed an ideal, as I hoped to leave the countryside, go to the city, struggle for myself, and search for everything I needed in life. This is the first thing I want to discuss: ideals.

SECOND, IT'S ONLY THAT . . .

Life has countless material and spiritual facets, countless beautiful and ugly elements, countless things that can and can't be told, countless yearnings that can and can't be realized, and countless ideals and visionary dreams (including the so-called Chinese Dream). However, the ideals that are most specific, most true, most widespread, and most representative are fame and longevity. We won't discuss longevity here because that is something that one can consider only after reaching a certain age. However, fame is a dream that begins to form as soon as people enter childhood and youth (or perhaps when they are still infants). One could say that for us so-called common people, an ideal would be to pursue fame and fortune during the first half of one's life and to pursue longevity during the second half. Meanwhile, in China enjoying fame and fortune is not merely a question of having a name, reputation, flowers, applause, and a continual flow of money; it is also a question of having a position and power.

When power symbolizes one's position, it can help yield fame and fortune, and for many people fame and fortune are synonymous with becoming an official. In becoming an official, one acquires power, and with power one acquires everything necessary for fame and fortune. This has been the iron law of life in China for millennia, and it is the most secular, most recognized, and most proven "truth." It is a secular law that has been realized in life. As for myself, in my youth and throughout my entire life, my spirit and pursuit have been constrained by these most secular of chains. Was this because I loved literature or because I loved power? When I was young, that was my biggest uncertainty. Because you love literature, it is only by continually writing that you can be promoted to cadre and be recognized as a civil servant—which is to say, a political cadre of the army. Therefore, you feel grateful to literature and come to love it. Meanwhile, your path to becoming a cadre and an official, and to being promoted from platoon leader to company commander and battalion officer, will be as smooth and unhindered as a stretch of street with only green lights. It is as though it would not be out of the question that in only two or three years you could be promoted to a regiment-level cadre. After all, just a few years after having been promoted to cadre, you've already become the military's most effective "literary spokesman." Power appreciates you the way the sun and spring breeze appreciate a tender sapling. At the time, I was appointed to serve as political instructor for a military company, and half a year later I was recognized as an "outstanding teacher-level grassroots cadre." Even later, I was assigned to serve as Party secretary and press officer at a military hospital, then became the hospital Party committee's "divine writing pen." Even later, I was transferred to the propaganda office of the army unit where I was stationed, and I drafted speeches and composed experiential documents. Although I wasn't the best writer in the propaganda office, I was the fastest and the most punctual. During that period, I would compose documents at work during the day and would write fiction at night. I was a military official by day and an author by night. My faith in the future was so strong that it was as if I had gotten fired up by taking steroids and stimulants.

It was also during that period that there was an incident that did not appear particularly significant at the time. Our army commander went to study at Beijing's National Defense University for a year, and the first thing he did upon returning to our unit was to wander through the barracks at sunset until he arrived at one of the family compounds. Because soldiers and military officials are people too, they still need to lead their lives, and almost every family in the family area raised chickens, ducks, and even large white geese. In the entranceway to virtually every home there were chicken and duck nests. Our family raised four ducks, which produced an average of two or three eggs a day. That evening the military commander came to the family compound to look around, and then he frowned, whispered a few words to a staff officer behind him, then walked away.

When the wake-up call sounded in the barracks the next morning, various officers from the family area—including bureau heads, associate bureau heads, officers, staff officers, and assistants—went outside to conduct their drills, whereupon they discovered that all their chickens, ducks, and geese in the compound had been poisoned. Some of the birds died in their nests, and others died outside. All four of our family's ducks had died outside the nest. One of them, when it saw me, feebly dragged itself over with its wings, and just before dying it quacked as though crying out, "Master, please save me!"

That morning, when the officers discovered that their families' poultry and pets had all been poisoned, virtually no one said a word. This is because everyone knew that this action had had been ordered by the commander himself.

That morning, when officers from the command department, political department, and logistics department performed their drills, no one said a word.

Moreover, the neatness of their uniforms and the precision of their movements resembled a military phalanx in Tiananmen Square. The commander stood solemnly next to the drill ground, as everyone silently maintained a powerful and unflinching gaze.

I had assumed something was going to happen that morning—that some sort of commotion was going to erupt out of that extreme silence. Therefore, my palms were drenched in sweat as I conducted my drills. However, when the drills were completed and the officers from the three major departments went to the commander to receive their instructions, the commander made no mention of the poisoned birds and animals. Instead, he solemnly praised everyone for the orderly and vigorous manner in which they had performed their drills. After he finished speaking, someone in the formation began applauding. Afterward, the unexpected occurred—on this day, the applause that followed the commander's instructions and praise to the officers was more orderly and vigorous than ever before, as though thunderclaps were obeying the commander's orders and were rhythmically erupting and raining down from the sky.

Afterward, it was as though nothing had happened. Whenever anyone saw the commander, they would stand at attention, salute, and smile just like before, and then exchange a few pleasantries.

I, however, found myself unable to forget this incident. Whenever I was reminded of it, in my mind's eye I would see that duck our family had raised for two years, struggling toward me and crying out, "Master, please save me!"

Afterward, you observed that whenever your fellow soldiers, colleagues, bureau heads, and associate bureau heads encountered the commander or other senior officials, they would invariably smile, stand at attention, and salute just as before. They would endeavor to exchange a few words with the officials—those elite power holders. Whoever the senior officials happened to address, and whoever they praised and encouraged, would be in good spirits for several days, as though their dreams had come true. If we approach this situation from a literary perspective, I must admit that I pitied them. At the same time, however, I was just like them; therefore, I also pitied myself. Of course, what someone does or doesn't do, what they abandon and what they retain, is almost never determined by a single incident, and instead it is the product of many different incidents. Whenever something suddenly occurs, it is invariably the product of countless other things that were either pursued or abandoned. My youthful pursuit and subsequent abandonment of money, fame, and power were the result of many different incidents. For instance, there was the time a friend and I secretly tried to start a business reselling musk, but things didn't work out, and my friend was seized and beaten by officers from the public security bureau, and in the end he was unable to have a wife and child, so he had to leave China for Romania. In retrospect, I understand that the poultry incident made me decide to give up my pursuit of money, fame, and power, as well as my obsession with becoming an official. After expelling these delusions like viruses, I found that my only remaining ideal was literature.

After wavering between loving power and loving literature, I eventually settled on loving literature.

I decided to devote myself to literature, and not to the power of which I was in awe and which I deeply feared.

At this point I, like a peeled onion, was left with literature as my only ideal.

After you were left with literature as your only ideal, writing became your sole focus and reading became your most interesting daily activity. Therefore, as you approached your thirtieth birthday—and as Confucius famously said, at thirty, one begins to stand firm—you began to devote yourself to writing. At that point, you could finish a short story in a single night and a novella in a week. You were a veritable writing machine. When a publishing house released your collected works in 1995, you took the opportunity to reread your previous works and discovered that although by that point you had already written several dozen novellas, they were all simply variations on the same story, and although you had created more than a thousand fictional characters, they were all simply variations on the same character.

You were shocked—shocked at your own repetitiveness.

You were stunned—stunned to discover that even when you thought you were moving forward through the literary space you had created, in reality you were merely marching in place.

Describing your own writing, you once declared: "Virtually all my writing is garbage!" Publishing is just a waste of paper, and reading is just a waste of time. You reflected on these questions and on the phrase "I believe." You considered the revolutionary literature that was featured in contemporary China's Red Classics, and when you compared it to nineteenth-century realist literature, you found that what the former most lacked was the individual author's sense of "I believe." Those novels' thought was generated by politics, revolution, and ideology, and was not the author's own. The fictional characters in those stories had all been approved by politics. They were all standard characters with the same size, height, skin color, clothing, and hair style, not the singular characters that one typically finds in works of world literature. Those novels did not contain any trace of the authors' "I believe." Even in the highly individualized language that many authors use, there is no "I believe," much less any distinctive story, characters, fate, thought, or writing method.

Meanwhile, when we recall the great authors and works from nineteenth-century world literature, we find that they all have their own "I believe," although they also leave us with a vague sense of dissatisfaction. For instance, there was a period when I felt that the greatness of nineteenth-century literature lay in familiar factors such as the works' characters, fate, and story, their rich and complicated inner world, and their magnificent social background. Of course, they also each had their own literary language. Compared to twentieth-century literature, however, these nineteenth-century works left me rather dissatisfied because in twentieth-century literature the author's "I believe" has already mastered and integrated nineteenth-century literature's "I believe." It has already broken through the author's "I believe" that had been shaped by characters, fate, inner being, story, and historical background. In twentieth-century literature, you find the author's own individual "I believe," whereas in nineteenth-century literature there is only an "I believe" that is collectively shaped by the author, readers, and critics.

Why do readers (or at least Chinese readers) view Tolstoy's and Balzac's works as the twin peaks of nineteenth-century literature? It is because within the literary consensus, these two authors have attained the highest level and unity. However, twentieth-century literature no longer shares the same "I believe," and instead it replaces the existing literary consensus with the author's own "I believe." The formation and development of different literary movements are the product of an author using his own attitude toward writing, and in the process rescuing and liberating the literary consensus (or collective) "I believe." This is a process both of breaking through and building up.

In Kafka's writings, the author's highly individual "I believe" rescued him and opened up a more fundamental authorial "I believe."

As for Camus's writings, it is not so much that they are examples of existentialist literature but rather that they are manifestations of the author's literary "I believe," which in turn established his own distinctive "I believe."

Virginia Woolf, Samuel Beckett, Marcel Proust, and William Faulkner, together with the Black Humor and Beat movements from American literature's golden age, followed by Latin American authors such as Jorge Luis Borges, Gabriel García Márquez, Mario Vargas Llosa, and Alejo Carpentier—their collective greatness lay in the fact that each of their works revealed, in the most complete fashion, the authors' own "I believe."

Virtually all twentieth-century literature is a display of the authors' "I believe"—a veritable treasure chest of "I believe."

We can also consider C. T. Hsia, whose *A History of Modern Chinese Literature* established him as the most respected literary historian in the Chinese-speaking world. When we discuss this study, we invariably observe that Hsia rediscovered Eileen Chang and Shen Congwen, as well as Qian Zhongshu's *Fortress Besieged*. It is as though if it hadn't been for Hsia, then Shen Congwen and Eileen Chang would never again have seen the light of day. However, Hsia also devoted a large amount of space to analyzing and promoting Zhang Tianyi, so why is it that Eileen Chang and Shen Congwen are currently so hot that they light up the sky, while Zhang Tianyi remains largely overlooked? Hsia also expressed considerable reservations about Lu Xun, yet Lu Xun remains widely read and discussed. Therefore, although our respect for Hsia's *A History of Modern Chinese Literature* undoubtedly derives from his rediscovery of Eileen Chang and Shen Congwen, I like the study not because of which specific authors Hsia promoted and critiqued but rather because his literary history contains his own distinctive "I believe."

Without Hsia's clear and courageous "I believe," we wouldn't have this respected volume of literary history, and conversely without this literary history's "I believe," there might not have been the acclaimed C. T. Hsia.

Given that this is how literary history unfolded, how can current and future literary fiction not also be like this? If a work doesn't feature the author's most distinctive and individual "I believe," it won't be literature, and it will be nothing but the author's tomb and coffin.

FOURTH, A GOOD NOVEL . . .

There is no fixed standard for what constitutes a good novel. However, once a work is recognized as being good, its canonical significance is virtually assured, like classics such as Homer's epics, Dante's *The Divine Comedy*, the Bible, and Tang poems and Song lyric poetry.

It is not the case that you first have readers' understanding of canonical literature, after which you have the author's works, followed by works that meet the readers' standards. Instead, good works are created in the absence of prior standards, and it is only after works are found and embraced by readers that they thereby come to be recognized as good literature. Reading and study are the beginning of the process through which literary works are recognized as good literature. Regardless of whether reading generates study or study leads to reading, an author remains oblivious to both. For an author, there is only writing. Authors rely only on their understanding of good literature (their "I believe"), and in this way they can write good works.

From Dante's *Divine Comedy* to Shakespeare's plays, Cervantes's *Don Quixote*, Goethe's *Faust*, and countless other classic nineteenth-century works—each work was created in a context in which authors didn't know what good literature was. These works' greatness is rooted in the way they conformed to their respective era's view of what is good. At the same time, the standard of greatness to which each work conformed continued to change during subsequent periods, though without denying the earlier eras' determination of what was great and canonical. For instance, although Tolstoy looked down on Shakespeare, this hardly affected the canonical status of Shakespeare's works. By the twentieth century, however, eighteenth- and nineteenth-century literature's characters, stories, fate, inner being, and writing methods came to be viewed as rather simple and old-fashioned, whereas twentieth-century authors were all creating their own writerly "I believe" with their own distinctive banners, methods, and isms.

You could say that in twentieth-century literature, the essence of the novelistic method was the essence of the novel itself. If that is true, then might the twenty-first-century standard for good literature undergo further change? Might we not come to view the twentieth century's isms as rather excessive or simplistic?

Will twenty-first-century authors' "I believe" continue to follow a twentieth-century trajectory, or will it instead respond with resistance and new awareness? Advance and retreat, awareness and betrayal, construction and deconstruction—for today's authors, this is all a mystery. Without a doubt, today's authors have no idea what the twenty-first century's good literature will be, but they do know that the twenty-first century's good literature *should not*—and indeed *cannot*—be identical to the nineteenth- or twentieth-century's good literature. Currently, an author's "I believe" appears particularly urgent and difficult. Because we now find ourselves at the beginning of a new century, where one century's literature abuts another, our understanding of what is good literature is therefore particularly mysterious.

Unlike the new "good literature" of the nineteenth and twentieth centuries, no one knows what form the twenty-first century's good literature will take. The new century's good literature will need to be explored like a labyrinth. It is because of this that writing can have significance, literature can become immortal, and authors can have an unquenchable passion. Everyone's assessment of good literature—be they authors, readers, or critics—is necessarily grounded on a preexisting foundation. If an author wants to write a good work, this will also be grounded on a preexisting foundation, although their standing and intention may be undetermined, confused, and unknown. Therefore, all the author's efforts will be established on a basis of their own "I believe" and will be for the sake of future writing. It is also for this reason that some authors know that they can write a good work today and therefore assume that they know what good literature is, whereas others are constantly seeking and revising their "I believe" and consequently never end up writing anything that they perceive to be good.

FIFTH, MY IDEAL IS SIMPLY TO WRITE WHAT I BELIEVE TO BE A GOOD NOVEL

I am fifty-five years old, which is a very melancholy age. Based on my assessment of my physical condition, my family's hereditary characteristics, and the fact that writing often wears me out, I can't imagine by the time I reach seventy I'll still be able to walk briskly, think clearly, and write nonstop whenever I sit down. This is simply how life is: when you are young and don't yet know anything, your body is still healthy, but by the time you finally start to gain some understanding of the world, you will have already begun to enter your twilight years. Even if you still feel like an able steed tied to a post, the sun inevitably will have already begun to set. Life is not a spectacular sunset, but rather it is just a melancholy red glow. To tell the truth, I find it hard to imagine that I could even make it past sixty or sixty-five. However, if I don't have an accident and manage to preserve my health, I'll continue attempting to face people's hardships with resilience, as I do in *The Four Books*, and tell stories with passion, irony, and humor, as I do in *The Explosion Chronicles*. This is not to say that *The Four Books* and *The Explosion Chronicles* were necessarily well written, but rather that I currently find myself writing more and more poorly. Given the realities of time, age, and fate, I anticipate that, barring unforeseen circumstances, I probably have no more than five or ten more years of good writing in me. And in those remaining years, will I be able to write three or four more good novels? This is my greatest worry, my greatest trepidation, and my greatest uncertainty. That is why, even now, I still haven't managed to settle on a definite "I believe" and instead constantly find myself in a state of uncertainty, doubt, and experimentation.

My writing is constantly wandering through a state of doubt and uncertainty. In this state of wandering and searching, I remembered Zhuge Liang in *Romance of the Three Kingdoms* and his six expeditions to Qishan, in which he used wooden oxen and horses to transport food and grain. *Romance of the Three Kingdoms* does not specify how these wooden oxen and horses were actually constructed, but in my hometown there is a legend about how Lu Ban, China's god of carpentry, dreamed of using wood not to construct houses and furniture but rather to create life. It is thanks to Lu Ban's skill that today we have beautiful houses, buildings, furniture, and tools, but his greatest dream was to use wood to create life—to create wooden oxen that would be able to plow the fields without needing to graze, and wooden horses that would be able to pull a cart without needing to eat. This was humanity's earliest dream of a perpetual-motion machine. Lu Ban struggled year after year, decade after decade, to figure out how to create these real live wooden oxen and horses, and because by the end of his life he still had not managed to find this secret, he therefore resolved to spend another lifetime searching for it. One day when he was old and disease had already spread to his vital organs, as he was lying on his deathbed bemoaning the fact that his lifelong efforts to create wooden oxen and horses had failed, a deity appeared before him and deposited into his brain a set of blueprints for creating the wooden oxen and horses in question.

Lu Ban immediately transferred these plans to paper; then he departed this world with a smile on his face. Our hometown legend holds that the blueprints that Zhuge Liang used on the battlefield are ones that had been handed down by Lu Ban's descendants for generation after generation. Zhuge Liang ultimately managed to establish and consolidate the Kingdom of Shu, but this would have been impossible without the wooden oxen and horses that he constructed from Lu Ban's blueprints.

Now I return to the issue of my writing. During the limited time I have left to write, the fact I still don't have that fully new, fully beautiful sense of "I believe" is undoubtedly because I still don't possess the equivalent of Zhuge Liang's blueprint for making wooden oxen and horses. As for Lu Ban, he spent his entire life designing a blueprint for wooden oxen and horses, but after he finally succeeded at the end of his life, he was still unable to create the actual oxen and horses that he wanted to give to the world and the people he so loved. Just think—could Lu Ban not have regretted the fact that, at the end of his life, he was unable to create his wooden oxen and horses? His regret must have been as great as a mountain and as deep as the sea, to the point that the living will never be able to experience a similar emotion. However, writing is a very personal activity and involves a process of unlimited amplification of the self. From this perspective, it is also the process of achieving the greatest realization of an individual's value. Therefore, I hope that during whatever might remain of my peak writing period, I may manage, like Lu Ban, to design a blueprint for wooden oxen and horses that would allow me to find my newest, most beautiful "I believe." I also hope that, like Zhuge Liang, I may eventually succeed in creating a literary version of his wooden oxen and horses.

This is why I would also say that my greatest ideal is simply to write a work that I believe to be good.

That is all; that is all.

Let me use some lyrics from a popular Buddhist song to serve as a conclusion:

Put down all your harvest,
Take back all your expectations.
Remember the relatives who love you,
Thank the neighbors who help you,
Greet your friends with a bow,
Kneel before the land that has nourished you.
That is all, that is all.

12 A Village's China and Literature

THE GEOGRAPHY OF A VILLAGE

The village where my mother, father, grandmother, grandfather, elder sister, and brother-in-law lived was like a plant that is indistinguishable from all the other plants in a vast wasteland, or a few grains of sand that are no different from all the other grains of sand in a vast desert. When I was growing up, the community was a large village with almost two thousand residents, but now it is a super-sized village with a population of more than five thousand. The community's recent growth has been a result not only of births but also of an influx of immigration. Just as people from around the country flock to Beijing and Shanghai, and people from around the world flock to America and Europe, people from throughout the region all flocked to our village.

Several decades ago, our village had a market street, and on the fifth day of every month people from dozens of *li* away would come for market day. Today, that same street has become a lively commercial avenue, like Beijing's Wangfujing Avenue, Shanghai's Nanjing Lu, Hong Kong's Central District, and New York's Broadway. Our economy, culture, politics, and folk art are nurtured, developed, and implemented on this avenue and in that village street. With contemporary China's crazed urbanization, our village has already become a town—in fact, it has now become a local capital, the same way that China's capital is Beijing, Japan's is Tokyo, England's is London, and France's is Paris. Therefore, it is not difficult to understand the village's prosperity, expansion, and modernization.

As I've previously discussed, the reason that the Chinese name for China is *Zhongguo*, meaning "Central Kingdom," is because in ancient times the Chinese believed that China was the center of the world. Moreover, China's Henan Province was originally called *Zhongyuan*, meaning "Central Plains," because it is in the geographic center of the country. Given that our village is in the center of its county, which in turn is in the center of the province, that means that our hometown village is in the center not only of the province but also of the nation and even of the entire world. This was Heaven's greatest gift to me, and it was as though God had given me a key to open the gates of the world. If I understood my village, that would mean that I understood the entire nation and even the entire world.

After realizing, one night when I was young, that our village was the center of China and that China was the center of the world, I felt a jolt of naive but real excitement—because I clearly felt I was living in the most central coordinate in the world. Moreover, I wanted to locate the center of the village because that would be the precise center of the world. One evening and deep into the night, I began calculating the distance from the eastern, western, northern, and southern ends of the village. At the time, my family lived on the western edge of the village proper, but because of the community's expansion, many people had built houses even farther to the west. Based on my calculations, and accounting for these new housing developments, I determined that the center of our village was our own house—and specifically, the entranceway to our courtyard. If our village was the center of the world and the entranceway to our house was the center of the village, didn't this mean that our house was the center of the center of the world? Didn't this mean that our house was the central coordinate of this great globe?

Upon realizing that our house, the area in front of our house, our neighbors, and our entire village were the center of the world, I became excited and uneasy, desolate and sorrowful. I was excited because I had just discovered that this was the center of the world, but I was uneasy because I felt that people at the center of the world would inevitably bear a greater responsibility. I felt that this might be a dark and difficult honor—the same way that in the center of a volcano there is an even hotter core, and in the deepest depths of the ocean there is an even colder stratum. If our home was in the center of the world, this must entail an even more extraordinary experience and burden. I was excited because at that time I was too young and ignorant, and simply couldn't believe that I had found the center of the world. I was worried others would doubt me, or even scorn and mock my discovery.

Meanwhile, I felt desolate because apart from myself, no one knew that our village was in the center of the world. I felt sorrowful on behalf of our village, like an emperor who has been secretly reduced to a commoner. I felt sorry for everyone else in the world because they had been living, working, and raising families for thousands of years without knowing the location of the center of the world in which they lived—as though every day they passed through the doorway to their house without knowing whether the doorway faced east or west.

That evening, in the still of night and under a sky filled with a water-like moonlight, I stood alone in the entranceway to my house and stared up at the sky, like the protagonist in *The Little Prince* standing on the surface of his planet and gazing out into the cosmos. I felt frustrated because I didn't know how I could convince everyone that our house and our village was in the center of the world, and felt sorrowful because of this secret that I had to keep.

EVERYDAY LIFE IN OUR VILLAGE

After confirming that our village was the center of the world, I noticed that everything in our village appeared extraordinary, and even the events of surrounding villages became mythical and legendary.

For instance, kindness and simplicity were common virtues in all of China's villages, but in ours this reached an extreme. During the Cultural Revolution, starvation and revolution pressed down on everyone's head like a pair of mountains. At that time, a young woman fleeing hardship arrived in our village, and because she was mute and had some cognitive deficiencies, people would therefore offer her their best provisions whenever she went to their house to beg for food. Seeing how well our village treated her, the woman proceeded to settle down in one of our village's wheat-field shacks—positioning her in our production team, or what today we'd call a villager group. We viewed this woman as a fellow villager, a neighbor, and even a relative. Whenever a family had a celebration, they would make sure to save her a bowl of food and an extra-large steamed bun. Whenever it snowed, a family that was relatively well-off would take a bowl of good food to her shack.

When it was cold, people gave her blankets, and when it was hot, they brought her blouses. When people were washing their clothes, they would wash hers at the same time. I don't know how this woman viewed our village—how she viewed the kindness and honesty of this community in the center of the world—but I felt that our village's virtue could serve as a mirror for the entire world. This woman lived with us for several years, until one day people realized that she was pregnant. No one knew who the father was, but a group of village uncles and aunties gathered in the street with clubs and axes and vowed that they would find the rapist and beat him to death.

Needless to say, their search ended in failure.

Afterward, the villagers pampered the woman even more, caring for her as though she were their own pregnant relative. They sent her eggs and flour, and when she was about to give birth, they helped find her a midwife. She successfully gave birth to a little girl and raised the child for over a year, but then one day she and the child suddenly disappeared. Half the village gathered around that empty shack, sighing and sobbing as though it was their own relative who had disappeared.

This was an ordinary yet also rather extraordinary story, the simplest illustration of humanity's emotion and kindness. Our only regret was that we forgot that the woman was still young and that she also needed love, affection, and a man. Perhaps her child was the crystallization of this affection and love. After I grew up, I often regretted that it hadn't occurred to the villagers to introduce her to a man so that she could settle down in the village and truly become one of us.

Kindness, beauty, and love—this is the ground on which humanity relies. In this village in the center of the world, this kind of ground, which resembles the foundation of a building, could be found blooming everywhere and was as common as home-style cooking. Every time I think back to that period, I feel as though I'm awakening from a dream, as though I had easily found the most desirable, beautiful, virtuous, and wise woman in my life.

Of course, that village—that territory—was the center of the world, and everything that occurred there was not, and indeed it *could* not, be the same as elsewhere. The village was like an extraterrestrial, whose behavior, words, and deeds could not possibly be the same as our own.

In the early eighties, during China's Reform and Opening Up Campaign, rural areas became more prosperous. The first person in our village to become rich wanted to buy a car, so he went to Shanghai and purchased a Santana. He then drove the car an entire day and night to bring it back to our village. At that time, the only person in our community who owned a car was the county head, but now even this ordinary peasant had one. When the peasant parked his car in front of his family courtyard, the entire village came over to observe it, just like the first time they saw a television. On that day, however, it suddenly started raining. The rain was unusually strong and continued nonstop for an entire day and night. When the car's owner got up the next morning, he found that the road in front of his house had been inundated and the bridge had collapsed.

From that day forward, that Santana never again left the man's family courtyard. It remained parked there forever, becoming a permanent souvenir of that era.

Time is always moving forward, just as a river is constantly flowing downstream. A nearby village suddenly became rich, becoming a model for how to help the poor become wealthy. The provincial governor and Party committee secretary repeatedly came to observe the village, after which bank loans began to pour in. To help the rich become even richer and to make sure that everyone knew how good this new socialist village was, the community spent its own money to film a television program, which was then given a prime slot on CCTV (and I should note that I was one of the program's scriptwriters). To demonstrate that they were in fact rich and to bring glory to our county, our province, and even the entire nation, the villagers also took out a loan to purchase a couple of small airplanes. The planes were nicknamed "Little Bees," and the plan was to let visitors fly around over the area so that they could observe the greatness of socialism. By paying just a hundred yuan, passengers would be able to realize their Chinese Dream of soaring through the sky in a plane—such a beautiful vision and ideal. However, after those two Little Bees were brought to us by truck, assembled, and given a test flight, one plane's wing broke off, whereupon both planes were then covered in a tarp and were never seen again.

Afterward, that village went back to being poor.

In real life, there are always some things that transcend reality, while it is the most commonplace occurrences that possess the greatest depth and humanity. The villagers were, after all, the center of the center of the world. The enormous transformations undergone by humanity and the human heart were like lava in the depths of a volcano. Several years ago, when I returned to the village to visit my family, one of my cousins came over and told me that while all the other villagers were proceeding along the road to wealth, his own fate had been uneven and difficult, like a cliff without a path or a river without a bridge. He explained that he had gone to considerable effort to purchase a truck, and he had just managed to make some money hauling goods when he accidentally struck a cyclist. The cyclist was a young woman, and her five-year-old son was riding on the back of her bike. When the bicycle was hit, the boy fell off the back and died before they were able to get him to the hospital. My cousin complained that he was the most unfortunate person imaginable. This is because, in that region, whenever there was this sort of accidental death, normally the culprit would have to pay only a few thousand yuan in compensation, and the case would then be closed. After all, given that it had been an accident, and furthermore everyone in that region was kind and understanding, there were even some cases in which the culprit would not have to pay anything at all, and instead the families of the culprit and the victim would become good friends. However, it turns out that the woman my cousin ran over—this mother who had been so full of life—was not so "kind" and "understanding," and instead she insisted that my cousin pay her thirty thousand yuan in compensation.

The loss of a life and the payment of thirty thousand yuan in private compensation, together with my cousin's sorrow and lament—this all left me speechless, and even now, years later, I am still unable to understand the transformation that our region has undergone.

I know that this village at the center of the world is no longer what it once was. It has changed along with the rest of the country, as everyone struggles to advance and not look back. For the sake of money and desire, everyone is losing their beautiful ethics, morals, and ideals, as the simple spirit that people once possessed is quickly being hollowed out and fragmented. This change has further reinforced the village's status as the center of China and of the world. Because the entire nation resembled our village, having lost its spiritual life and become controlled by materialism and a desire for money, it is as though the entire world has become like this, with materialism trumping everything.

More importantly, this kind of spiritual loss has already become a way of life. It has become as commonplace as the sun rising in the morning and setting in the evening. It has become a custom, a habit, and a blood-like regional culture. For instance, the region's abundant forests were chopped down by poachers, whereupon the forestry department developed and introduced a genetically modified species of tree—a new kind of poplar that could be harvested in just two years. After the village's original several dozen species of trees had all been replaced by this new species, it was as though the millions of different species of animals in the world had suddenly been replaced by a genetically modified species of pig that could reach maturity in just two years. This was such a terrifying new reality!

Moreover, people now like to steal. With a family like mine, people assume we're rich because I'm an author, and one year we were robbed four times. In that village it was not only my family that was robbed but virtually all families perceived as being rich. Perhaps this was a Chinese-style Robin Hood redistribution of wealth, but whatever the reason, the sorts of robberies that people used to disdain have now become a daily occurrence.

It is these changes in daily life that are the deepest form of change and that are also most representative of this center of China and of the world.

CHINA IN THE VILLAGE

If our village's ordinary activities, daily necessities, and minor household affairs cannot be said to be the community's most Chinese characteristic, then let's instead consider the village's response to major affairs. What are China's major affairs? They are none other than politics, power, foreign relations, and war.

First, let's discuss politics and democracy.

In the early years of the People's Republic, rural grassroots cadres organized democratic elections for people to elect the village head. One year, there were two candidates for the position of village head of this community in the center of China. One candidate went door-to-door canvassing for votes, and at each house he would offer gifts and ask how everyone was doing. The other, meanwhile, rented out a couple of beef and mutton soup restaurants one morning (people in our village love to eat beef and mutton in the morning), and invited everyone to drop in and eat, drink, and even take some food home with them. The result is that it was the latter candidate—the one who spent more money and was perceived as being more generous—who was ultimately elected. I describe a similar situation in my novel *The Explosion Chronicles*.

Our village Party secretary is elected by the village's Party members. My elder brother was a Party member, and every time there was an election for village Party secretary, he was always so terrified that he didn't even dare return home because the candidates for election would come looking for him and invite him out to eat and drink, in hopes that he would vote for them. As a result, whenever there was an election, my brother would go into hiding to avoid this democratic process, and if something came up and he had no choice but to return home, he would sneak back in the middle of the night.

He once said to me, "Why do we need democracy? Democracy has transformed me into a thief and has made it so that I'm not even willing to see anyone."

Next, let's discuss political education.

Political education is a big thing in China. Currently, it is not enough that you have a political awakening; more importantly, you must remain in accord with the center. I recently returned to our village for a visit, and as I was walking down the street, the village head suddenly ran over. I assumed he was coming to greet me, but to my surprise when he saw me, he exclaimed, "You've returned? You must immediately go home. I need to go study a document from the general secretary on contacting the mass line. I have to make sure I remain in accord with the center and can't afford to deviate from it even for a single day."

I was stunned.

I wanted to laugh.

I also had a deep sense of panic. I knew that ever since the Cultural Revolution, political education in China has almost never relaxed. Even in this remote village, the situation was still just like during the Cultural Revolution.

Third, let's consider our village's views on war. War is the most extreme form of national power, politics, and foreign relations. Based on our village's understanding of war, one can appreciate the core of many big and important matters.

For as long as I can remember, among the people in our village who have had a chance to see the world, the national matter that interests them the most is war, and particularly the questions of when Taiwan will be liberated and whether China could defeat the United States. Several years ago, back when First and Fourth Uncle were still alive, whenever I returned to the village, I would always sit next to their sickbeds as they held my hand and asked me to explain national events and the international situation. They would ask when we would liberate Taiwan and whether China could defeat the United States. Of course, I told them that we would liberate Taiwan very shortly and that we could certainly defeat the United States. I explained, however, that the reason China had not already liberated Taiwan is because the Taiwanese are, after all, our compatriots, and if China were to attack Taiwan, countless Taiwanese compatriots would surely be killed. I explained that this was why Taiwan had not yet been liberated and suggested that a peaceful liberation would still be the best option. I also explained that it would not be difficult for China to deal with the United States. Given that China has nuclear weapons, if necessary, it could simply launch a few nuclear missiles at the United States, and the US problem would thereby be resolved.

First Uncle, Fourth Uncle, and the other villagers all believed me.

Upon hearing my assurances, they had renewed faith in the people and felt more love for the fatherland.

Meanwhile, everyone in our village is currently concerned about the Diaoyu Islands. They curse China's leaders for being too timid and stupid, saying, "So who are the Japanese? If we send them a couple of nuclear bombs, wouldn't that clear everything up?"

This was our village's perspective on politics, war, power, and foreign relations, and this was our village's view on democratic freedom and human rights. If our village's affairs were to be expanded, they could be China's affairs, and if China's affairs were to be shrunk down, they could be our village's affairs. Therefore, one could say that this village was the most real China, just as contemporary China is the most real version of our contemporary village.

OUR VILLAGE'S LITERATURE

Does this village—which is in the center of the world and is almost equivalent to China—have any literature?

Yes, of course it does. Not only does it have literature, but furthermore its literature has no peer. Its literature is great, and its artistic value is unprecedented. If the world's greatest authors and works were to be placed in that village, they would appear tiny and insignificant. If the world's most modern and innovative literary works were to be found in the village, they would appear old, traditional, and outdated. Meanwhile, if the world's classics—including works like Homer's epics, *One Thousand and One Nights*, *The Divine Comedy*, *Don Quixote*, and Shakespeare's plays—were to be found in the village, they would not appear to be traditional and backward but instead modern and advanced.

For instance, Franz Kafka, regarded as the father of modern literature, was highly respected by virtually all twentieth-century authors. However, a thousand years ago our village already had a legend about reincarnation and rebirth, in which someone was supposed to be reincarnated as a pig or a dog but went through the wrong door and was born as a human. One day when this person was asleep, a deity transformed him back into a pig or a horse. This story is from a thousand years before that morning Gregor Samsa woke up as an insect.

When I was young, I knew of a villager who had "cat-eagle eyes." He couldn't see a thing during the day but could see perfectly at night, and the darker it got, the better his eyesight became. Therefore, he knew about everything—including everyone's secrets, sexual affairs, robberies, and thefts. His eyes were like a pair of searchlights illuminating all the village's secrets. This miraculous and magical phenomenon was much more real than any of García Márquez's magical realism.

Dante's *The Divine Comedy* is a classic, but our village has its own legends of Hell and Purgatory that first appeared two thousand years before Dante and that were far more thrilling and enlightening than *The Divine Comedy*. Cervantes's description of the windmill battle in *Don Quixote* is certainly very moving, and it is Spain's most vivid spiritual symbol. In our village, however, there is a legend of a battle between a millworker and a millstone, in which the millworker attempted to use his strength, resilience, and perseverance to make the millstone turn continuously until the stone's ridges were worn smooth and the stone was completely worn away. The millworker shouted to the millstone that only after the stone conceded defeat would he stop turning it.

Dostoevsky's *The Brothers Karamazov* has a plotline in which Jesus himself, pretending to be an ordinary believer, comes to hear a priest's sermon and observe people's confessions. When I first read this novel, I trembled with astonishment when I reached this section. Later, however, I observed that among the residents of our village, their most insignificant religious behavior is far more moving and shocking than this scene. For instance, in our village there was an illiterate old woman in her seventies. She had never been to church, nor had she ever gone to a temple to kowtow and burn incense. She had never married or had children, attracted little public attention, and spent her time planting crops, growing vegetables, weeding, raising chickens, sweeping the courtyard, and harvesting autumn fruit. It was as if she didn't even exist, and no one even remembered the most extraordinary events of her life. However, regardless of whether it was China's atheistic Cultural Revolution period or the materialistic Reform and Opening Up era, every morning and night she would make sure to stand in front of her window and silently pray to a miniature cross made from a pair of chopsticks.

For decades, this old woman had been praying every day to that homemade cross. The piousness of this woman who had never seen the inside of a church was far more intense than the faith-related plotlines of classic works like *The Brothers Karamazov*, *The Scarlet Letter*, or *The Power and the Glory*. Every time I'm reminded of this woman, my heart aches.

When I think back to all the great, rich, sorrowful, and joyous stories I've read about in books, I realize that they've all already occurred in that village, and furthermore in the village they were all more real and more shocking than in novels. It is only on account of my stupidity that I was not able to recognize the existence of the stories in my village. I've seen too much of that village's streets, houses, fields, and seasons, as well as people's daily activities and life events. I was submerged by that village's daily life and its Chinese-style physical, material, and physiological life, to the point that I overlooked the village's art, which transcended physical, material, and spiritual existence. I've been writing for more than thirty years, but it is only now that I've gradually begun to realize that my hometown village is one of the world's greatest literary works. Even if all the world's literary works from throughout history were combined into one, they would not be able to surpass the literary value of my hometown village.

Although our village does not have the equivalent of the extravagant architecture of the Grand Prospect Garden that appears in China's great novel *Dream of the Red Chamber*, our village has its own versions of all the work's characters. Jia Baoyu, Lin Daiyu, Xue Baochai, Wang Xifeng, and Granny Liu all lived in our village. Although the legends of *The Classic of Mountains and Seas* and the Mountain of Flowers and Fruits in *Journey to the West* do not appear in our village, they are nevertheless intimately connected to our land. Li Bai wrote countless poems while sitting in the mountains in front of our home. Bai Juyi and Fan Zhongyan felt that my home's scenery and climate were favorable, which is why they were buried in the soil of my hometown. Our hometown is truly a literary heaven, a Grand Prospect Garden containing all literary characters and stories. However, not only do I lack the ability to write them down; I don't even have the ability to discover, realize, or imagine them.

My ignorance derives from my limited understanding of that village and that territory—the same way that our perception of a desert's dryness derives from the fact that we lack a green oasis in our hearts. But now, when I realize that our village is a literary oasis in the middle of a vast desert, my age, life, and destiny limit my ability to traverse that desert and enter that oasis. Now that I recognize that our village is truly a great work of world literature, and I understand that it is an island in a vast ocean and a grassland within a vast desert, I am already well on my way on an irreversible route in the opposite direction.

OUR VILLAGE'S READERS

To have literature, one must have readers, the same way that to have art, one must have art lovers. Because of the individual, collective, and national nature of people's behavior in this village, their daily thoughts and the spiritual dimension of their existence belong not only to literature but specifically to serious literature—pure "bright sun and white snow" literature, definitely not the kind of mass literature and popular literature that outsiders idly peruse. Only popular authors and artists can find comedic and meaningless elements in their own lives. It was from this sort of village that China's great author Lu Xun made most of his deepest observations and realizations. Shen Congwen and Xiao Hong also took inspiration from this sort of village. Because of this, when the people from this village become readers, they have no interest in reading Lu Xun, Shen Congwen, and Xiao Hong. If you say that Lu Xun's *The True Story of Ah Q* is good, they'll reply, "What's so good about it? Isn't my neighbor just like Ah Q? You feel that Xianglin Sao is the most pitiable and sympathetic person in the world, but we feel that the woman living across the street is even more of a Xianglin Sao than Xianglin Sao herself, and is even more deserving of compassion, sympathy, and assistance." Over the past century, there has been no shortage of figures in our village who are comparable to Lu Xun's Old Chuan and Kong Yiji, and if Xiao Hong's Little Cui is beautiful, then are not the girls who wash clothes in the river in front of our village similarly beautiful? What is worth seeing about the streets, ponds, gardens, and myriad of living beings in *Tales of Hulan River*? Which village and family is not already like this?

Everyone who complains about peasants or who says that the village doesn't have culture or readers is wrong and biased. It is not that the villagers don't have readers but simply that they don't read "bright sun and white snow" literature. The reason that they don't read pure literature is because their lives and behavior are *already* pure literature. Conversely, why do they like to read works like *Romance of the Three Kingdoms* and *Water Margin?* It is because the life and spirit of these two novels are the precise opposite of their own and the novels' stories have a high degree of popularity and vulgarity. Why do they like to read *Journey to the West?* It is because the plotlines in *Journey to the West* are 108,000 *li* away and include things that could never occur in their own village. The same way that most people like to read things that are unfamiliar to them, that contain a hint of familiarity, or that contain an element of familiar unfamiliarity — the same way that we read William Faulkner, Albert Camus, Ernest Hemingway, Alain Robbe-Grillet, Italo Calvino, Jack Kerouac, Milan Kundera, and Philip Roth, and works like Somerset Maugham's "Miguel Street," Orhan Pamuk's *Snow,* and Ismail Kadare's *The General of the Dead Army.* The reason why villagers like to read these works is because they find them simultaneously familiar and unfamiliar. At this level, people from our village are literate and cultured, but they don't read books by Lu Xun, Shen Congwen, and Xiao Hong because they are already too familiar with the characters and plotlines in those works. The reason they read Jin Yong and old-style martial-arts novels is because they lack these sorts of stories and plotlines in their daily lives. They watch *The Pearl Princess* and other palace movies and television series because even in their dreams they'd be unable to come up with those sorts of settings and plotlines. For people in this village, it is the effect of familiar unfamiliarity that plays the decisive role in deciding what they will read and watch.

Otherwise, what is most surprising is that although the villagers don't read Lu Xun and Shen Congwen, they are nevertheless very fond of Tolstoy, Dostoevsky, and Hugo. In the mid-eighties, after I joined the army and left my village, I returned to the village and found that the village's young people were enthusiastically passing around the novels *Anna Karenina* and *The Hunchback of Notre-Dame,* to the point that the books became dog-eared and tattered, and eventually the villagers wrapped the cover of each book in kraft paper. After they finished these novels, they sighed and exclaimed, "Ah, so this is how foreigners live!"

With respect to this village's readers, they feel they have no need to read works that directly describe their souls. From this perspective, every great author owns their own piece of land and village, so if they want the people from their village or their land to read their novels, they will find that this is a useless and impossible task. The residents of the fictional Yoknapatawpha County have no need to read William Faulkner's *The Sound and the Fury*, and they would rather read *Gone with the Wind* and watch Westerns. Readers in the Caribbean have no need to know that English author Graham Greene and Colombian author Gabriel García Márquez have already written about their region.

The greatest failure of Chinese author Zhao Shuli is that he hoped the residents of his hometown territory would read his novels—he wanted to write for them. Conversely, his greatest achievement is that he did not achieve his wish. That the people from his hometown did not want to read his novels is precisely his success. Similarly, like the residents of Lu Xun's fictional Lu Town, the residents of contemporary Shaoxing are proud of Lu Xun, but they are not willing to read his works.

People whose souls have been dissected are not interested in seeing their own soul blood—this is literature's most basic rule. Herein lies the greatest error in Mao Zedong's "Talks at the Yan'an Forum": Mao wanted literature to describe workers, peasants, and soldiers, while also wanting workers, peasants, and soldiers to read these works that were written about them. The result was inevitably nothing but drifting smoke and empty slogans. What happens in literature and what happens in real life have no real connection to each other. Therefore, for villagers not to read Zhao Shuli is, in fact, a compliment to him. The people from that village are the best readers in the world—because it is they who best understand the relationship between literature's essence and their own lives.

THE RELATIONSHIP BETWEEN THIS VILLAGE AND LOVE

To tell the truth, I'm rather famous in this village. You could even say that everyone knows me. However, I'm famous not because I wrote some novels and essays, but rather because they all know I'm an author and can earn enough in royalties that I'm able to comfortably support my mother and my two sisters, who still live in the village. More importantly, because I'm famous, our county head and Party secretary, as well as the town mayor and Party secretary—they all have college and graduate degrees and are well-informed readers—feel that I've brought glory to our hometown. So when I return home, they all come to see me or else invite me out to eat, and when they are bidding me farewell, they'll say to me in front of all the other villagers, "Lianke, if you need anything at all, just tell us!"

In this way, I've become a famous personage in our village, and even the county head and the town mayor come to my home to see me. The other villagers don't care what I've written or whether it is well-written, but for me this is all very important. The result is that I continually return to the village to claim and "steal" content, although the village itself knows virtually nothing about this. The village is an inexhaustible fountain from which I draw literary inspiration, and even if I take one, ten, or a hundred pails of water from that fountain, the fountain won't care because it is continuously flowing, day and night. Conversely, if I don't take water from the fountain, the fountain will overflow and the water will disappear.

I have become that village's perpetual claimant.

I have become that territory's son who doesn't need any reciprocation.

But what did that land want me to do? My parents birthed and raised me there. Like them, when I was young I experienced endless happiness and hardship. Even today, these experiences continue to give me that spiritual nourishment that I need for my writing—all the emotions, frustrations, pain, joy, and sorrow. They grant me all the stories, plotlines, language, and feelings I need—to the point that when I'm traveling around the world, even the topics of my so-called lectures are drawn from that village. What, then, do the villagers hope that I'll do for them in return? For thousands of years, they've experienced difficulties and vicissitudes. However, they don't need someone to speak for them because they feel that experiencing hardship is one of life's necessities, to the point that if one doesn't experience hardship, could one even be said to be alive? Nor do they need anyone to describe and recount their innumerable happinesses. Those happinesses are the compensation for their hardships and the necessary result of their conquering hardship, the same way that if peach and plum trees can manage to make it through the spring, they will bear fruit in the fall.

Accordingly, I continually draw content from that village and keep writing, writing, and writing, while also narrating, narrating, and narrating. Was it really for the sake of fame and fortune that I became an author who is known throughout China and perhaps even throughout the world? If so, then what does that village, which has given me more than thirty years of stories and plotlines, want me to do? Moreover, these different stories and plotlines; histories and realities; birth, aging, illness, and death; time and place—they are like a literary warehouse that opens only to me, or mother's milk-filled breast that opens only to me. Over many, many years, there have been countless thoughts and turns—the same way that after waiting for thousands and thousands of years, and searching for thousands and thousands of *li*, in the end the Dalai Lama was selected as the reincarnated Buddha, will I similarly be selected to become an author of that village and of that territory? Let me experience, feel, perceive, and think. Let me use my most individual method to recount all sorts of different stories, characters, and innermost joys and sorrows that will never be able to leave that village or that territory. In the end, what are that village and that territory for, and what do they illustrate?

It is only now, after having been writing for more than three decades, that I finally realize what this village, this land, and these people are for and what they illustrate. It turns out that they are not for anything and do not illustrate anything; instead, they exist only so that, after I have been selected to write, I might thereby use them to prove that the village and this piece of land are the center of China and the world.

It was decided that I would use literature's reputation to bear witness to the fact that they are the center of the world.

All my writings are evidence that our village is the center of the world. The better I write, the more powerful this sort of evidence becomes; the more individualistic and artistic my works become, the more permanence that this evidence will have.

That's all. Because the villagers endured such hardship to select me, I must do my utmost to repeatedly prove this point.

Afterword
Ripping Open the Dreamscape

Upon learning that the English edition of *Sound and Silence* would be released to the world, I felt like I had just been punched in the heart by Mike Tyson. Neither pleased nor upset, I was simply muddled and confused—as though confronted with an unexpected development that I had no choice but to accept. That night I tossed and turned, unable to sleep, and I kept wondering, if today I were to receive a similar invitation to give a series of lectures at North American universities, would I still proceed to stand in front of the students with a sheet of paper in hand while happily prattling on and on?

I'm afraid I wouldn't.

If not, then what would I say?

I don't know.

All night, I lay in bed in my apartment in Hong Kong's Clear Water Bay, simultaneously restless and meditative, but also feeling as though my mind were in a fog. In this weak, sensitive, and apprehensive state, I surveyed the freedom and calmness that had produced the sorrow and entanglements of my life. My spirit was forever a whip I was brandishing at my own soul, and my writings are merely scars left behind by that whip, while those moments of humor, ecstasy, and joy that readers find in my novels are but the self-mockery and self-soothing gestures of a self-flagellating masochist. Even today, I can't bring myself to reread the casual remarks that are recorded in *Sound and Silence*, and I can't even remember what exactly I said in those lectures.

Even though I can't recall the exact content of those lectures, the volume still makes me feel very restless and uneasy.

It is as though all of this were merely a dream of time.

It is as though all time were merely a dream.

Authors are but people who can rip open and peer into that dreamscape.

This set of lectures from more than a decade ago is merely a set of confessions and explanations resulting from that earlier process of tearing open and peering into the dreamscape. However, today's reality is completely different, and virtually no one can glimpse the innermost reality that lies hidden in the depths of the current dreamscape. Today's dreams have become as vast as a mountain, and whoever wants to shatter their hard shell would need bloody fingers and spiritual instruction, yet it is precisely for that reason that the resulting writings would be valuable and meaningful. However, the limits of my current age and life force leave me powerless when confronted with these hard-shelled dreams. I often wonder when I should finally put down my pen and go in search of a peach-blossom spring where I could spend the rest of my days, never again engaging with issues relating to contemporary China and its people, and never again concerning myself with worldly affairs.

I often wonder, which will be my final work?

When will I finally be able to create a dream for myself?

Given that *Sound and Silence* is a collection of a decade-old set of confessions about a ripped-open dreamscape, what is there now for me to rip open, peer into, and confess about? I really can't say. Every day I write as though I'm not writing anything at all, and I run around like a bee that flies blindly but is unable to produce honey. Compared to my situation at that time, my current understanding of literature has now completely changed, as has my understanding of contemporary China and its people. Perhaps someday I'll write a new volume of confessions, or perhaps I'll instead be like a bee that is unable to produce honey and instead forever flies around blindly. Who knows? Perhaps the significance of writing and speaking is that they yield a set of riddles and proverbs we use to describe a time that we'll never be able to crack open, yet it is because of these riddles and proverbs that we must continue to read and write. The fact that Carlos offered me the opportunity to give those lectures a decade ago and that Duke University Press has now given me this opportunity to distribute these confessions to people in the English-speaking world—this reminds me of that ancient yet familiar sentiment at the heart of Chinese Buddhism:

Oh, myriad beings, remember the kindness of others, and you will possess everything.

Biographies

YAN LIANKE is the author of *Discovering Fiction, Heart Sutra, Hard Like Water, The Day the Sun Died, The Explosion Chronicles, The Four Books, Lenin's Kisses,* and many other works of fiction and nonfiction. Winner of the Franz Kafka Prize and twice a finalist for the Man Booker International Prize, Yan teaches at Renmin University in Beijing and the Hong Kong University of Science and Technology.

CARLOS ROJAS is professor of Chinese cultural studies at Duke University. He has translated a dozen books by Yan Lianke, including *Discovering Fiction* (Duke 2022).

Index